Your Towns and Cities in the Great War

Kensington
in the Great War

Your Towns and Cities in the Great War

Kensington
in the Great War

G.I.S. Inglis

Pen & Sword
MILITARY

First published in Great Britain in 2014 by
PEN & SWORD MILITARY
an imprint of
Pen and Sword Books Ltd
47 Church Street
Barnsley
South Yorkshire S70 2AS

ISBN 978 1 78303 288 4

Printed and bound in England
by CPI Group (UK) Ltd, Croydon, CR0 4YY

Typeset in Times New Roman by Chic Graphics

Pen & Sword Books Ltd incorporates the imprints of
Pen & Sword Archaeology, Aviation, Battleground, Discovery,
Family History, History, Maritime, Military, Naval, Politics, Railways,
Select, Social History, Transport, True Crime, and Claymore Press,
Frontline Books, Leo Cooper, Praetorian Press, Remember When,
Seaforth Publishing and Wharncliffe.

For a complete list of Pen and Sword titles please contact
Pen and Sword Books Limited
47 Church Street, Barnsley, South Yorkshire, S70 2AS, England
E-mail: enquiries@pen-and-sword.co.uk
Website: www.pen-and-sword.co.uk

Contents

Introduction

When one thinks of Kensington in 1914, one envisages broad streets and grand houses full of servants. Certainly the central and southern parts of the Royal Borough included plenty of these, as well as Kensington Palace and salubrious Kensington High Street, with its great emporia like Derry & Toms, Barkers of Kensington and Ponting's. Despite all the evident wealth, there was considerable poverty, especially to the north in the Notting Dale and Kensal New

Page from Walker's 1914 London street-map covering almost all of Kensington Borough, apart from the very south. The shapes at the extreme left of the map are the layouts of the White City exhibitions. (A)

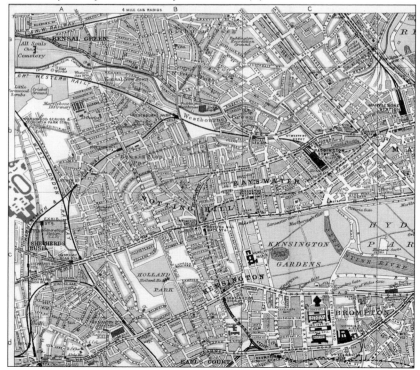

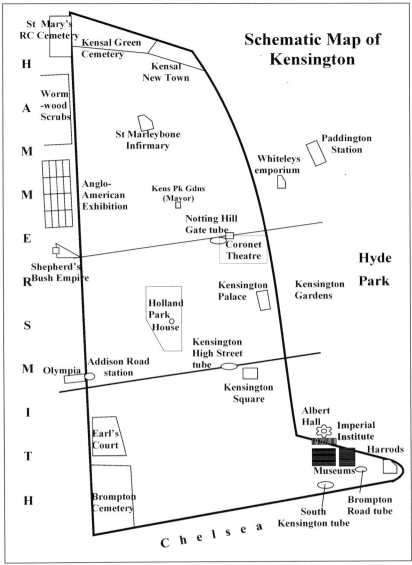

Schematic Map of Kensington to show the main areas mentioned. (A)

Town areas, with overcrowded multi-occupied dwellings, while slums could be found hidden behind and even among the large houses.

One commentator said in 1903: 'Northward above Notting Hill is a very poor district, poor enough to rival many an East End parish'. Thus the death rate for 1914 in Norland Ward (north) was 20 per 1000, over twice that in Brompton (south) at 9 per 1000. So looking at Kensington as a whole, its infant mortality rate for 1913 was actually higher, at 112 per 1000, than neighbouring Hammersmith, Fulham or Paddington (each around 100).[1]

I have used the approximate physical boundaries of the Royal Borough to represent 'Kensington', but what one might call mental borders are seldom precisely identical. Thus Kensington Gardens and the Albert Hall are quintessentially Kensington, but are in the Borough of Westminster.

The Borough has been described as a boot pointing to the right. At its top we have the huge Kensal Green cemetery, where famous Victorians such as Brunel, Thackeray and Trollope were buried. Starting at the top, we soon reach Kensal New Town, an area of particular over-crowding which used to be part of Chelsea until 1900. We move approximately south down the boot until we reach Notting Hill Gate (home of the Coronet theatre, with the giant William Whiteley's emporium just outside the boundary and another giant store, Selfridges, further on at the beginning of Oxford Street). Next we encounter Kensington Palace and its grounds, then the South Kensington museums (with most of Kensington Gardens – plus the Albert Hall, Albert Memorial and the Imperial Institute – on the 'wrong' side of the borough boundary). At the tip of the toe we have

The Shepherd's Bush Empire, with its characteristic dome. (p-c, A)

The Anglo-American Exposition: The popular Indian Dance (101 Ranch).

Harrods' huge department store. Travelling around to the heel (with the Borough of Chelsea as the 'sole') we go westwards to find Brompton Cemetery and round to Earls Court and its exhibitions area. As we travel up the back of the boot we border the Borough of Hammersmith most of the way. First we encounter another famous exhibition area, Olympia. Further north we graze Shepherd's Bush, home of the popular Shepherd's Bush Empire, and also the entrance to the White City exhibition area. Here the Franco-British Exhibition was held in 1908 to celebrate the Entente Cordiale between the two countries. Many of its white-painted buildings were still extant at the time of the 1914 exhibition, the Anglo-American Exposition, with its working model of the Panama Canal, the Grand Canyon Railway and a Wild West Show among the attractions. Further north we pass the open area of Wormwood Scrubs on our left, and move through North Kensington back to St Mary's RC Cemetery (actually part of the Borough of Hammersmith) and the adjoining Kensal Green Cemetery.

The first and most famous of the White City exhibitions. (2008 Centenary Brochure)

The Anglo-American Exposition: to celebrate 100 years of peace between the countries. (WC)

Showing the crowds at the Anglo-American Exposition. (p-c, A)

Snippets from July 1914

The Dead End - flogging a dead horse. In July the Borough saw off yet another attempt by the London County Council to impose the hated tram upon Kensington. The terminus ('The Dead End') would remain at Shepherd's Bush Green:

> *Surely never since the dreadful days of the Steamboats fiasco has even the L.C.C. manifested a blinder crassness, a more headstrong persistence in kicking against the pricks, than in this attempt...to force its obsolete, obstructive tramway system upon portions of the Metropolis where it will be most unwelcome and unwanted.*[2]

Mrs Pankhurst carried off. Women's suffrage was one of the biggest issues of the day. The Women's Social and Political Union were the militant suffragettes, frequently in trouble with the police. The cycle would go: WSPU person does something outrageous, is arrested and sent to prison. There she goes on hunger strike. Using the new 'Cat and Mouse Act', the prison authorities release her before she becomes gravely ill. She recovers (often at Mrs Brackenbury's house, nick-named 'Mouse Castle' at 2, Campden Hill Square), but once she recommences her militancy, she is arrested again and so on.

A packed WSPU meeting was being held at Holland Park Hall. Miss Annie Kenney had made a stirring speech, while Mrs Dacre-Fox had

Trams were welcomed in Kingston – its mayor is driving the first one over Kingston Bridge – but not in Kensington. (WC)

been too weak to talk for long, but the guest of honour was absent:

> *The enormous building was filled by an audience whose enthusiasm, intensity and indignation was increased tenfold by the arrest of Mrs Pankhurst on a stretcher as she was being conveyed from a nursing home to the Hall. Mrs Pankhurst, who was in an exceedingly weak and emaciated condition, was accompanied by her nurse, who was allowed to go as far as Holloway Prison with her.*[3]

Law-abiding Suffragettes Arrested. The Women's Freedom League (WFL) had broken away from the WSPU, disapproving of its more extreme tactics. They set up a stall in Kensington High Street laden with home-made and home-grown produce to raise some money. Business was brisk until the police – perhaps believing that all suffragettes/

The Women's Social and Political Union (WSPU). (WC)

Annie Kenney at her most magnetic. (SE)

Mrs Pankhurst borne away again (this is outside Buckingham Palace). (WC, p-c A)

The government's counter against principled women starving themselves to death, or being force-fed, in prison. (WC)

Women's Freedom League: happy to be photographed in more relaxed poses: publicity shot from 1908. (SE)

suffragists were the same – suddenly swooped. Both the stall and the women were brought in front of a magistrate at West London Police Court. Mr Bryon was not impressed with the police case:

> *After viewing the barrow and assuring himself of its innocent contents, he discharged the smiling defendants.*[4]

New career opportunities for women. Progress towards the vote was still uncertain, but there were a few new career paths for women. Changes in retailing introduced by the large department stores meant that customers were encouraged to touch the products on sale. Of course shoplifting rose accordingly, so the department stores had to find clever ways of fighting back. At the West London Police Court,

Hannah Kelly and Rebecca Morris, both machinists, were charged with stealing 38½ yards of silk and fourteen silk scarves belonging to Barkers of Kensington:

> *The chief witness was Miss Annie Betts, an attractive, smartly dressed lady, who was employed by Messrs Madigan & Kemp, private detective agents…to attend a sale at Messrs Barkers for the purpose of bringing shoplifters to justice.*
>
> *Miss Betts stated that she saw the prisoners enter Ponting's shop (part of Barkers' premises) and owing to their suspicious conduct she kept watch on them. When they reached the silk department Morris picked up a roll of silk off the counter and put it under her coat. Afterwards they moved into another department, where Kelly snatched up some silk scarves and put them under her cloak. Witness communicated with the shop-walker, who followed them with her and assisted her to take them to the office. There they gave up the property they had stolen.*
>
> *The witness added that each woman had a large pocket running all round her skirt – "a professional pocket", added the lady detective. When she first caught hold of Kelly the prisoner said, "Take your hands off me. You ought to be a man."*
>
> *Kelly* [speaking from the dock, interrupted the witness]: *"I should think so. My arms are black and blue."*
>
> *Mr Garrett: "You apparently agree with the witness as to what you said."(Laughter.)*
>
> *Kelly: "It was like a navvy pulling me about instead of a woman."* (Laughter.)[5]

The cleansing of verminous children. Scarlet fever was the most common of the notifiable diseases, with numbers slightly up on previous years, but more Kensington Council time was spent on the verminous children problem, countered by renting premises at Mary Place in Notting Hill, installing the requisite baths and disinfecting chambers in them, and having school nurses send the children over to get treatment, costing two shillings per child per month, or 8d per bath.

An oily film on our lungs? There were too many internal combustion engines in the Borough of Kensington. Petrol engines had taken over

This garage, based in the High Street, is open day and night for its (rich) clientele, who might also seek to hire a car. (KN).

This garage is from the north (close to Whiteleys) and we note that deferred terms are available as well as driving instruction. (KN)

from horses, but there was the suspicion that they set up a vibration that could weaken the foundation of buildings. Also, as anyone could see the oily film that petrol engines left on the walls of buildings, what was it doing to our lungs?

Sir Ernest Shackleton about to Endeavour. Sydney-born Mrs Arthur Popplewell was one of London's legendary hostesses. Guest of honour

Shackleton, barely recognisable in unfamiliar naval garb, is on board Endeavour *and about to set off. (p-c, A)*

at her July garden party in South Kensington was Sir Ernest Shackleton, about to set off on what would become his most famous Antarctic expedition. He sang for his supper by contributing a rousing speech on exploration and adventure, but looked somewhat embarrassed at the two ugly golliwogs he was given as expedition mascots. On 4th August King George gave Shackleton a real mascot, a Union Flag, to take with him – and bring back safely.[6]

Mayor Foreman. (DG)

A change of name would soon be appropriate. The Mayor and Mayoress of Hammersmith, Mr and Mrs Foreman, held an at-home for friends and colleagues; not in their Kensington house, but their houseboat *Cigarette* at Hampton. In perfect weather, 400 guests were splendidly entertained, one of the successes of the days being the melodies of **Herr Meny's (White Viennese) Band**. Military bands were popular at such events, but there was no guarantee that '*Herr*' Meny was Austrian – many of his band members were probably British; while

A few pre-war gramophone records by Herr Meny's Band still exist.

the white simply referred to the colour of the uniforms. He was probably the *Monsieur* Phillippe R. Meny, whose *Belgian* Orchestral Band and Concert Co toured Australia in 1915, raising money for Belgian charities.[7]

Works Outing to Southsea. Rawlings Bros Ltd, of Gloucester Road, inventors of the rawlplug, had their works outing to Southsea. As luck would have it, the Fleet had been assembled that day for the King's Inspection, and one of the most popular jaunts was a voyage in a small boat around it. Later there was a dinner at one of the best hotels in town and many speeches were made:

> *In proposing the toast of "The Employees", Mr Rawlins spoke of them as being the best body of men he had ever met. He was well aware that they were not angels, indeed he was glad they were not, but for clean manliness, talent and industry, he felt they would be difficult to equal.*[8]

Clean manliness? Mr Rawlins must have been affected by the sight of all those sailors.

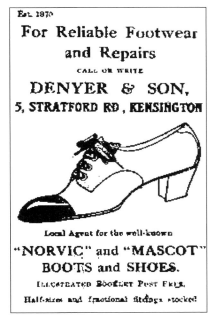

We note that back bacon from David Greig is just a shilling a pound at the beginning of the war. (KN)

One of the few advertisements to incorporate a picture: makes it stand out from the pack. (KN)

SHORT AND SONS, LTD.

Purveyors of English and Scotch Meat.
Irish and Wiltshire Bacon.
Dairy Produce.
Fish, Game, Poultry, etc., etc.

WE GUARANTEE——
  Highest Possible Quality.
  Careful Supervision of all orders.
  Prompt Despatch,
  Moderate Prices.

5, 17 & 19, High St., Notting Hill Gate, w.

Possibly the leading butcher in the Borough – we shall come across them again. (KN)

Last of the old Victorian firms? An old sign for the company, with 'Motor Body Works' stuck over something else, can still be seen high on a wall close to its old Spring Street HQ. (KN)

Situation Vacant, 31/7/1914. *'Invalid lady requires young gentlewoman; **German preferred**; as companion for afternoons. Address: Temple, Kensington News, 118, Church Street.'* It cost 6d for 14 words for one insertion, but many were tempted by the better value of three weeks of insertions for just one shilling. This one did not appear again, however.

CHAPTER 1

War

*Praising criminals for the self-control they are exercising
during the present period of stress and anxiety*

When war did come, it found Kensington as
well prepared as it could have been. Its
vigorous new Mayor, William Davison, had
presided over a recruiting campaign as far
back as February-March 1914 for the local
Territorial battalion (the 13th Londons,
Princess Louise's Kensington Regiment,
but often referred to as either The
Kensingtons or 13th Kensingtons). He had
campaigned in May for suitable headquarter
premises for the local battalion of the
National Reserve, while in May the whole
eight detachments of the local Red Cross
were mobilised to meet a notional sudden
arrival of war casualties in an Ambulance
Train at the local Addison Road Station

*William Davison, Kensington's
vigorous new mayor. (B)*

(now called Olympia), with the Vicarage Hall turned into a temporary
hospital.

By the end of July 1914 the crisis in the Balkans, following the
killing of the Austrian Arch-Duke Franz Ferdinand by a Serbian
assassin on 28th June, had deepened and seemed likely to suck in the
two main alliances, with Germany, Austria-Hungary and Italy (the
Triple Alliance) on one hand and France, Russia and Great Britain (the
Triple Entente) on the other.

His weekly copy safely deposited, the editor of *The Kensington News and West London Times* (hereafter *Kensington News)* bought tickets for his Bank Holiday long weekend in Brittany. On Saturday (1st August) the news was full of dire threats. It seemed prudent to stay in England, so he changed his destination to Felixstowe: a lucky choice for a journalist. On the way he saw railway stations still swarming with the usual Bank Holiday crowds – no one wanted to miss their holiday – but once at the coast he saw the Felixstowe-Harwich harbour full of destroyers and cruisers. On the Sunday his hotel was full of uniformed men, even taking over the dining room as a mess room. And he noticed soldiers outside the hotel guarding apparently innocuous roads and bridges: this was, after all, the nearest naval base to the likely enemy. On the Monday he saw sailors joining their ships amid tearful farewells – including the manager of the hotel, himself a reservist. Early on the Tuesday morning (August 4th) he was wakened by the sirens of the fleet as it slid out to sea. On the next day, after the declaration of war:

> *At noon we were listening to the boom of guns in the North Sea, and within an hour our pleasant hotel had been commandeered for a hospital and placid faced nurses, with the Red Cross badge, were methodically making preparations for the reception of the wounded. Since then that hastily improvised hospital has received the first of the wounded German sailors, and the inevitable horrors of war are being tempered by the mercy of humane, though resolute, British men and women.*

It was as a result of the first British-German naval engagement of the war. HMS *Amphion*, a light cruiser, led part of the Harwich destroyer flotilla in pursuit of the German minelayer, the *Königin Luise*. The

The Königin Luise *had been converted into a minelayer.*

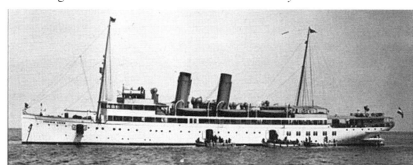

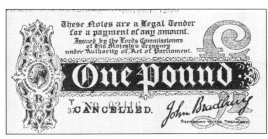

One of the strange new one pound notes. (Pageant)

GOD SAVE THE KING.

ARRANGEMENTS have now been made for the enrolment of Special Constables, to assist the Metropolitan Police in the protection of public buildings and preservation of order. All British citizens of good physique, resident in the Metropolitan area are eligible, but it is specially desired that no man fit for service in the Navy, Army or Territorial Forces shall apply. Special Constables will be expected to serve for a minimum of 4 hours out of every 24, and to give their services free of cost, but each Constable will be provided with the necessary equipment, consisting of warrant card, truncheon, armlet and whistle.

Applications for enrolment may be made on Monday next, August 10th, and subsequently from 8 a.m. to 10 p.m., at the nearest Police Station, where further information will be obtained.

The Special Constabulary is under the direction of Colonel Sir E. W. D. Ward, K.C.B., assisted by a staff.

August 8th, 1914.

Special Constables were sceptically regarded at first, but their reputation gradually grew. (B)

latter was eventually sunk at 12.22 pm but, early on the 6th, *Amphion* ran into mines the German ship had laid, and went down with considerable loss of life.

If there was singing and dancing in celebration of the war in Kensington, it was not commented on in the local newspaper. Instead it described the mood as one of 'quiet but grim determination' and said that this was the time for 'neither boast nor panic'.

Unfortunately, panic buying of food was almost immediate. The *Kensington News* again:

> *It became necessary in several cases for traders to literally barricade their counters to keep back the clamorous women who, if served with all they wanted, would have taken away the whole of the stock.*[9]

Prices shot up. The Bank of England avoided a run on gold by extending the Bank Holiday until the Friday and then issuing £1 and 10 shilling notes for the first time.

At a personal level, if you had run out of money over the weekend and were waiting for the banks to open Tuesday morning you would be out of luck, as happened to Dorothy Peel – journalist, expert in cookery and domestic economy, with a string of books published from 1898 onwards – who was stuck in Woking in a holiday let with only 2/9d to her name and keen to go back home to Brompton Square. No one knew her well enough to cash a cheque for her. Eventually a kindly grocer loaned her £3.[10]

Lord Kitchener was appointed Minister of War on the 5th and issued his famous appeal for a huge new 'special army' on the 7th. Both Kensington and Hammersmith councils enthusiastically backed the Prince of Wales's National Relief Fund, as whatever course this war took, there would be immediate loss of incomes and unemployment.

We can see this by looking at the Work Wanted and Situations Vacant columns for before and after the declaration of war. On 31st July the *Kensington News* featured sixty-one Work Wanted and seventy-six Situations Vacant Small Ads (fifty-two of these, ie 68%, being for domestic service). In the 14th August edition there were nearly twice the number of Work Wanted notices (114) and about the same total number of Situations Vacant (seventy-seven), but non-domestic service jobs had shrunk to fifteen (19% of total versus 32%).[11]

A practical example was the building and decorating trade: a director of Thomas Crapper & Co, the makers of sanitary ware in the King's Road, Chelsea, wrote immediately to the *Kensington News* to beg anyone to give work to his workers, as:

> *At this time of year the decorative section is usually at its busiest, but unfortunately, we hear on every hand of the withdrawal of instructions which had been given for work to be executed.*[12]

On a lighter note, the Shepherd's Bush Empire was quick off the mark to turn the war to its advantage: 'The latest war news will be shown by lantern slide from time to time at the Bush Empire.'

Thomas Crapper & Co, suffering at once. (KN)

Enemy aliens at Olympia. (THW)

Enemy aliens were rounded up and held in a compound at Olympia. Not all were gathered up in the first swoop, of course. Some were away from home, and others were none too keen to be found. A few advertised their presence in less sensible ways: Felix Seaboth, a German provision dealer of Portobello Road, was accused before Mr Garrett of disorderly conduct:

Britain's Motto:
BUSINESS
AS
USUAL.

But business was anything but 'as usual'! (KN)

> *PC Henson, 155F, stated that the prisoner was surrounded by a crowd of 300 persons. He was shouting that "One German is as good as ten Englishmen." Witness had a job to get him away from the crowd.*
> *Mr Garrett: "They were very angry, I suppose?"*
> *Witness: "Yes, sir."*[13]

Some immediately saw a profit in it: Chas P Harrington ('Auctioneer, Surveyor & Estate Agent') offered to look after any 'German, Austrian or Other Nationality' business until the end of the war.[14]

TO FOREIGNERS.
Germans, Austrians, and Others.

Those owing to the National crisis, having to leave their Business or Homes are invited to put their affairs under the Management of

Mr. Chas. P. Harrington.
Auctioneer, Surveyor & Estate Agent,
53. Shepherd's Bush Green,
who is prepared to watch their interests, whether large or small, until the War is over.

Shops Managed, Private Property Protected. Rents Collected.
Banker's References. Telephone 1452 Western.

One wonders how many takers he got and what happened at the end of the war. (KN)

The 13th Kensingtons were at their annual camp when war broke out. Despite the recruitment attempts of the Mayor and others earlier in the year, they only numbered 568 out of an establishment of over 1000. They quickly returned to London and began recruiting in the Town Hall. The latter was soon a veritable hive of activity, with Territorials recruiting in the vestibule and at the front entrance; the Council Chamber and Small Hall was set aside for Red Cross Training; National Reserve training was happening in the Council Members' Room; meals for the Territorials were being cooked in the basement. Besides these, there were lots of people milling around outside the Town Clerk's offices wanting to offer their services, to do anything, anywhere (but often without any special skills to match their enthusiasm).

Badge of the 13th Kensingtons. (A)

In a few days the 13th Kensingtons reached their establishment. On Sunday 9th they were joined by those in training as Red Cross nurses at an impressive Drumhead Service in Kensington Gardens, opposite the Palace, and in the presence of Princess Louise of Kensington, the President of the Kensington Division of the Red Cross. All then made

The Mayor receiving the Colours of the 13th Kensingtons after the Service. (B)

The 1/13th Kensingtons marching past the Mayor. (B)

... And the Red Cross Nurses. (B)

their way to the Town Hall, when the Colours of the regiment were handed over to the Mayor.[15] The Battalion and the nurses marched off 'amid loud and continuous cheering' to their Headquarters, the Drill Hall in Iveagh Gardens. When the soldiers arrived, their commanding officer asked them the key question, if they were willing to go to France on active service (they were not obliged to go abroad). Fortunately, 'practically all replied in the affirmative'.

A week later, on Sunday 16th, the Kensingtons marched to the Town Hall to say farewell to the Mayor before departing for training camp at Abbots Langley, where they joined up with the rest of 4 London Territorial Infantry Brigade. The departure was of course a tearful affair, but the men looked fit and ready.

As it neared the end of the month, news of the British Expeditionary Force's heroics at Mons greatly swelled the numbers of willing recruits. On the 31st recruitment began in Kensington for a second battalion of the 13th Kensingtons. As the Mayor noted, enthusiasm was so great on the first day that:

> *It was necessary to make them form a queue, which extended during the greater part of the first day from the Town Hall beyond the entrance of St Mary Abbots Church.*[16]

In fact it just took a few days to raise this battalion, numbered the 2/13th Kensingtons, to its establishment, and there appeared to be plenty more volunteers, so the Mayor offered to raise a battalion for Lord Kitchener's New Army.

News coming back from the war was heavily flavoured with anti-German propaganda and scare stories. German-bred racing pigeons were reckoned to be simply waiting for secret information to be attached to their legs before they would speed off to Germany. German-made goods were of course boycotted, people even warning of the 'flood' of Bavarian-printed Christmas cards to be expected shortly.

What was to become of theatres and places of entertainment? The Shepherd's Bush Empire, fearing that it might be closed down, as in Paris, used its advertising space to argue, citing former Prime Minister William Gladstone, that in times of anxiety 'the mind must be relieved from over-strain' and that 'Now more than ever, the Variety theatre is a necessity', while just to be present when the whole audience was singing the National Anthem was a truly 'soul-stirring' experience. In the autumn both George Robey and Marie Lloyd appeared at the Empire: top stars of the variety circuit, but the Empire's owner, Oswald Stoll, also owned the huge London Coliseum.[17]

Some of the first volunteers to go over to serve in France were London bus drivers with their buses – perhaps 300 in the first few weeks. Many large employers urged and even offered incentives to their male employees to volunteer for the Colours. Thus the London and South-Western Bank offered to pay volunteers their normal wages in full for three months, while Harrods offered each employee who enlisted a £2 bonus, with support for dependent relatives.

Every week the amounts donated by Kensington and Hammersmith to the Prince of Wales's Relief Fund were listed and were very close to each other in total. There was one critical difference, however. Although the majority of donations in both places were low

THE Prime Minister's Views.

GLADSTONE, who visited the Theatre on the night of the news of Gordon's death, said: " In the time of distress and doubt the mind must have relief in intellectual recreation, and the Theatre was the best form of recuperating the mind."

Now, more than ever,

the Variety Theatre is a necessity   It is not a luxury. To keep fit and meet, the calls our country may make, to help in one way or another, the mind must be relieved from over-strain.   There is no better mind-recreation than a weekly visit to the Shepherds Bush Empire, the "Coliseum" of West London.   All the latest War News and Special War Pictures on the Bioscope.

The National Anthem, sung by the entire audience

at all performances, is soul-stirring, and will be something to remember in days to come.   Come and help to sing it.

KEEP THE FLAG FLYING'   BOOK NOW.

Shepherds Bush Empire
6.30   9.0
THEATRE.

Telephone : Hammersmith 225 or 226.
For complete programme see page 4.

It was a masterstroke to make use of the National Anthem experience. (KN)

WHAT THE BUSES ARE DOING
No. 200

Some are at the front.

Some have been transformed into motor-lorries for transport.

Some are working as hospital vans at the naval ports.

Some are away in the country doing odd jobs at Territorial camps.

Some are engaged collecting up and removing German prisoners.

Some are conveying wounded soldiers from the stations to the hospitals.

Some are engaged in meeting and distributing war refugees.

Some are on the street carrying on their usual business.

BUSES ARE THE MOST USEFUL OF ALL VEHICLES

DO YOU WANT A BUS?

Then Telephone Victoria 8700 or write the Private Hire Department, London General Omnibus Co., Ltd., Electric Railway House, Broadway, Westminster, and we will do our best for you.

London buses were indeed versatile, as the London General company (LGOC) were not shy in telling everyone. (KN)

London buses and drivers were quickly pressed into service (From Peace to War).

value affairs, such as £1, or 6/7d collected from pupils at a school, or even the occasional £20 from a church collection, when it came to large donations these tended to be from rich individuals in Kensington but from companies and factories in Hammersmith. In fact the most generous of these was the Osram-Robertson lamp factory in Hammersmith, donating £210 per month. Possibly they felt they needed to be whiter than white because they had some German shareholders (due to complicated patenting reasons). Companies were very sensitive about being thought to have German connections; thus J Lyons, the famous caterers of Cadby Hall, Olympia, were suing Lipton Ltd, their rivals in the tea market, for libel for that very reason.

It was 9th September before the Mayor received permission to begin recruiting for his New Army battalion. It would be a 'Pals' Battalion, which is to say that people who joined together would be able to serve together: thus seven people joined from Whiteleys store in Queensway: all were placed in the same company and even the same platoon within it. He quickly organised a launch meeting in the playground of a new LCC Notting Hill school for the next night in which he and

ACTION FOR LIBEL.

J. LYONS & CO., Limited (Plaintiffs)

v.

LIPTON, Limited (Defendants).

IN the HIGH COURT OF JUSTICE Mr. Justice Sankey, on September 8th, 1914, granted an Interim Injunction restraining Lipton Limited, their Agents and Servants, from speaking or publishing or writing and publishing any words to the effect or of the substance that J. Lyons & Co., Limited, or the Directorate thereof, is composed of Germans, and that by purchasing their commodities the public is assisting the enemies of Great Britain.

J. LYONS & CO., Ltd. (By Appointment to His Majesty the King)

IS AN

ALL-BRITISH COMPANY

WITH

ALL-BRITISH DIRECTORS,

HAS 14,000

ALL-BRITISH SHAREHOLDERS,

AND 160,000

ALL-BRITISH SHOPKEEPERS

SELLING

LYONS' TEA

Cadby Hall,
Kensington, London, W.

Lyons were most upset at being accused of being German controlled. (KN)

And some London buses got themselves captured by the Germans. (IWN)

patriotic local MPs like Alan Burgoyne MP (and his Liberal rival FM Carson, happy to be on the same platform) and Lord Claud Hamilton MP beat the recruitment drum. The Mayor's speech was particularly impassioned:

> *Why are we fighting? The German Chancellor gave the true reason to our Ambassador. "You are going to fight," he said, "for a little piece of paper." Yes, we are fighting for a little piece of paper, but by that little bit of paper England's honour was pledged. To what? To protect the weak against the strong. To protect right against might. (Cheers.) What would have been our position to-day if we had stood aside and withdrawn from our bond for fear or greed of gain? What would have been our feelings if we had looked at gallant, heroic Belgium, laid waste by barbarian hordes? ...As the Prime Minister said, "It were better that our country were blotted out from the page of history." (Cheers.) Assuredly our cause is righteous. We strove for peace and we were given a sword. And now we must see his thing through. (Cheers.)*

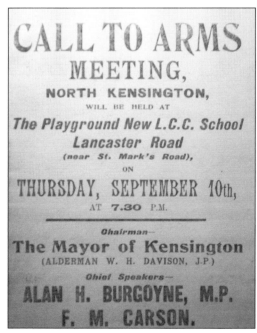

Mayor Davison managed to get 11 of Kensington's most prominent men on the platform at very short notice. (B)

The scrap of paper obliging us to go to the aid of Belgium. (THW).

... The War Office asked me if I could help them with their new army. I said, "Yes, if you will let me have a Kensington Battalion where those who know one another can be trained and serve together." They said, "If you can raise a battalion of 1,100 strong you shall have the honour of calling it the Kensington Battalion."

I am therefore asking you to fill up the forms which can be had at the table, by which you undertake to enlist for the duration of the war...

And should it be that some of you who go forth shall be added to that great Roll of Honour of those who do not return, still I say to you:-

Haste Ye! Enrol!

"For how can man die better than facing fearful odds
For the ashes of his fathers, and the temples of his gods?"
(Prolonged cheers.)

Once the other speakers had stoked the fires still further, a 'fairly large number of recruits' was then enrolled.[18]

There was a problem however; within a few days it was evident the anticipated numbers just were not coming in. We know now that recruitment had already peaked and many of the men who had been inspired to join the Colours by stories of Mons had found somewhere else. Then, however, the Mayor and his colleagues redoubled their efforts. Meetings were held all over the Borough. The Borough of Hammersmith was roped in: they hoped to

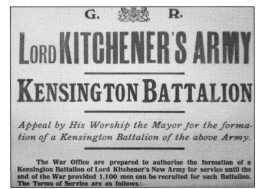

(Part of a) Recruiting poster for the Mayor's battalion. (B)

provide up to two of the four companies required. The Northampton Polytechnic (in Regent Street) was also encouraged to have a recruiting station and they hoped to raise a company. It was to no avail, and numbers slowed to a trickle somewhere about the halfway mark. There was another problem. Colonel Arthur du Cros MP (and others) had been raising a battalion of colonial Infantry at the White City (meant to be composed of men from the colonies who happened to find themselves in London). The recruiters for the latter were not above pinching those recruits generated by the publicity created for the Mayor's Battalion. They, too, were about halfway to completion. Major-General Sir Francis Lloyd (in charge of London forces) now made the sensible recommendation to merge the two half-battalions to make one full battalion. The Mayor was astute enough to have the other half added into his battalion, so it could still be called 22nd Royal Fusiliers (Kensington).

So the Kensington Battalion was born, a unique mix of colonials and Londoners. A and B Companies were the colonials, most of whom were from the dominions: Canada, Australia, South Africa etc, but some people had come from places such as Buenos Aires and Chicago. What the colonial companies brought was an enterprising, outgoing frame of mind. As the colonial recruiters had cast their net over theatre-land and the West End they had a number of gifted performers in their ranks, so the Battalion concerts would become a fondly-remembered part of the initial training period.

C and D Companies were the original Mayor's Battalion recruits. They were split roughly by social class so that people would feel comfortable with like people around them: D Company received most of the middle class men: from banks, major retail stores and so on, while most of the working class men went into C Company: men from Notting Hill and to the north of the Borough, or outdoor workers from the Council, like Chris Wakelin and Bill White and their rugby pals, the four brothers Smith.

This story shows most of the issues:

He was a very amiable recruiting sergeant, the day was a Sunday in September 1914, the date the 13th, and the place was the White City, Shepherd's Bush.

There had been a war on for a month or so, but the doctor did not think my chest measurement quite good enough for the Army.

The recruiting sergeant asked me as I was leaving how I had got on and seemed very surprised at my fate.

He requested me to wait, and after he'd had a few whispered words with the recruiting officer, I was invited to try my luck with the doctor again.

By some chance or other, my chest measurement was by then satisfactory and I was then returned to the recruiting officer who kindly asked me what regiment I would like to join. I replied that any old lot would suit me.

"We have a very fine regiment of Colonials in formation at the White City," he said, and I was invited to join them. I could hardly claim to be a Colonial, but I was assured that, being anxious to become full-strength as quickly as possible, this regiment was willing to take a few other than Colonials on holiday in England, of which it was proposed to form the regiment."[19]

Fred Pignon volunteered in slightly different circumstances:

'Jack Greenslade and I worked for a well-known news agency in 1914. Our assignments included reports on the queues of young men scrambling to join Kitchener's Army. One day Jack said to me: "Why aren't we among these blokes?" I couldn't think of an answer; so we hied off to Kensington rather than Whitehall, interviewed a smiling Irishmen in the Mayor's Parlour [Mayor Davison was an proud Ulsterman] *and a few minutes later had taken the King's Shilling, drunk a glass of champagne and were on our way back to Fleet Street to tell our editor, who took a rather dim view of his errant reporters, now soldiers.'[20]*

Private Bill and the two Mabel Faheys in September 1915. The younger Mabel is just a month old. (Courtesy Bill Fahey)

Bill Fahey lived in Southam Street in the Kensal New Town in the very northern edge of the Borough. Aged 21, he had just married his sweetheart, the beautiful Mabel, on 6th September; but he worked for the Gas, Light and Coke Company at their gasworks just off Ladbroke Grove and this was a very patriotic company, many of whose young men had already joined the 13th Kensingtons.

Bill found himself being badgered by the older men to join up. Being

Fanciful sights encountered 1: The original caption reads: 'Old gentleman engaged in quiet siesta in Kensington Gardens suddenly wakes to find himself in the above alarming situation and hastily concludes that the Germans have arrived.' (Punch)

assured he would get his old job back was possibly the clinching factor and he signed up with the Mayor's Battalion.

Most of the Fusiliers Battalion stayed at night at the White City, while doing most of their daily training in Wormwood Scrubs, near the

Fanciful sights encountered 2: The sorts of fanciful sights encountered by new recruits at the White City. (A)

prison: marching up and down the football pitches and manoeuvring past the goal posts. Maurice Drake commented:

> *All around the bare barrack sheds and dusty parade grounds are the lath and plaster glories of the White City: pink and white columned facades; grotesque towers and pinnacles snowy white against the pale autumn sky.*[21]

One of the most incongruous volunteers was a chap called 'Dad' Grover, over-age but still determined to do his bit. Although a private, he was from a well-off family (his father was a lieutenant colonel) and he turned up in a chauffeur-driven Rolls Royce every morning. He would in fact make it out to France as a stretcher-bearer.

Meanwhile Princess Louise had visited the 1/13th Kensingtons in their training area at Abbots Langley, where an officer told the *Kensington News*:

> *Fifteen miles a day – good hard marching. That's what we've been giving the men lately. Our first duty is to make them physically tough, capable of standing any amount of exposure, able to march until the soles of their boots drop off. This war is proving again that the army that marches best is the best army.*[22]

The 2/13th Kensingtons, now commanded by the man who had done sterling recruitment work for all three Kensington battalions, Major now Lieutenant Colonel McLean, were doing their initial training in the grounds of Holland House. Most men, being local, were able to go home at night.

Other visitors seen in Kensington were around 200 Belgian refugees, who were billeted in the Kensington Workhouse (now officially called an 'Institution') – not the sort of address the Belgians would have desired, but it was only until they could be found other homes, and locals rallied round with books, money, clothing and so on. We hear rather

The peppery Lt-Col McLean, who had helped with the recruitment of the 1/13th, 2/13th and the 22nd Fusiliers. (TK)

First there were sad little family groups, like this wounded Belgian refugee and his family from Louvain. (THW)

Then larger numbers. Here (at the Workhouse) we have gramophone entertainment and nursing staff on hand. A Belgian flag is held aloft, but everyone is still cowed and shocked. (THW/ Media Storehouse)

less about locals rallying round with comforts for the 128 German, Austrian and Hungarian aliens in the Mary Place Institution, but the latter seemed reasonably happy with their stay:

> *Some thought their circumstances were somewhat hard, but admitted that during a state of war such a condition of things must necessarily exist.*

In fact the Master said that they had been very well behaved on the whole, and most of those who were of military fighting age were shortly moved on to the larger compound at Olympia.[23]

After two months of war, people had settled into inconveniences like censorship, shortages and pubs now shutting at 11 pm (later it would become 10 pm). They continued to subscribe to the Prince of Wales's Relief Fund, now augmented by Queen Mary's The Queen's Work for Women Fund to help the large number of women who had lost employment because of the war. It was noticeable too that certain privileges for uniformed men that had been offered in the excitable days at the outset, such as free or half price underground travel or theatre entry, were being quietly withdrawn. There was one piece of good news: crime had gone down by 40 per cent, with the Chairman of the London Sessions praising criminals for:

> *The self-control they are exercising during the present period of stress and anxiety.*[24]

Louis McCausland was a well-known local figure. He joined the army aged 14, and had completed 28 years of service by the time he retired in 1898. Now he was General Secretary at the Kensington Hospital and trained the local National Reserve Battalion in his spare time. He was released from his duties to knock the Kensington Fusiliers into shape. He was totally unlike the traditional Sergeant-Major:

> *You remember, there was not much of him; short, stocky and smiling, he was the most loved Sergeant-Major in the British Army...with a heart*

Louis McCausland, the first RSM of the 22nd Fusiliers (pictured in 1915 after he had been obliged to take a commission). (P-A)

of gold and an encouraging smile which was far more effective than the raucous ravings which are supposed to be the adjuncts of a R.S.M. [Regimental Sergeant-Major] *Can't you hear him now "Why do you worry me so?" as we tried our damnedest to look and drill like soldiers back in 1914.*

His other favourite trick involved having the men lined up in front of him and asking:

There are nine hundred and ninety-nine men doing their best – and one man spoiling the whole Battalion – why will you punish me?

– and convincing each person that they were that thousandth man that was letting everyone down.[25]

As it turned into autumn, thoughts turned to the annual mayoral elections. Mayor Davison was here, there and everywhere: it was hard to think of anyone better; surely he (with the same logic for Mayor Foreman in Hammersmith) could be persuaded to stand again? 'Carillon' from the local paper watched the Mayor in action:

A peep into the Mayoral parlour the other day revealed to my astonishment the heavy burden in this unprecedented time. It represented a combined busy commercial office and Army catering store. The Mayor, with an anxious eye on the clock, was giving audiences to the members of his battalion and others, and his secretary [Mr G.A. Hames], *with a look of having endured sleepless nights and laborious days, was exerting himself to his utmost to keep up with the accumulation of business. As soon as he had dismissed one visitor, another was there to claim the Mayor's attention; several stood at the entrance waiting patiently for their turn. This goes on up to late in the evening. The Mayoress looked in and inquired if her husband could be home to dinner at eight o'clock. He was unable to assure her of that.*[26]

His Kensington Fusiliers Battalion probably took up most of his time. The problem was that while he had been able to help the 1/13th and 2/13th Kensingtons reach their establishment and leave the rest up to the Army, the War Office's interpretation of 'raising a battalion' meant that the raiser supplied it with all the necessary equipment apart from weapons. This meant khaki tunics, marching boots, greatcoats, kitbags, distinguishing badges and many other items.

Of course, even if the raw materials were available, there would be no one who could manufacture the items. All companies working on war materials were grossly overworked and understaffed. This was where the Mayor's extensive list of contacts and his clout as the Mayor of the Royal Borough came in. By applying directly to the Managing Director of Harrods, the latter were somehow able to rustle up for him the last khaki in London. Harrods were also persuaded to take on a number of the other requirements, particularly the boots. Derry & Toms, another large Kensington retailer, supplied a number of the others – including some superb Kropps razors, selling at half-price. Lillywhite Frowd, more used to making cricket pads, were persuaded to try their hand at marching equipment (packs, webbing etc).[27]

Some of the last khaki in London, conjured up by Harrods. (B)

It was another thing to get the companies to deliver on time; in the Mayor's papers are many letters saying you promised xxx items delivered by *this* date, and it is now *that* date and we have only received xx (or none at all). Thus Colonel Innes writing about delays in the receipt of shirts from Derry & Toms; 1,200 shirts ought to have been delivered over a fortnight earlier, but only 708 had arrived:

These shirts are very urgently required. There are 350 men who have not received one; and many of those issued have already been in wear 10 days and it is quite time they were washed.[28]

Paul Rubens, composer of the
song and later engaged to its
singer before consumption
forced him to withdraw.
(Daily Graphic, B)

The lovely Phyllis Dare.
(p-c, A)

THE MAYORESS OF KENSINGTON
(Mrs. W. H. Davison)

requests the pleasure of your company at

an ENTERTAINMENT for

The Kensington Battalion The Royal Fusiliers

On WEDNESDAY, OCTOBER 14th, 1914, at 8 p.m.

in the Grand Restaurant (close to the Garden Club),

at THE WHITE CITY, SHEPHERD'S BUSH.

Entrance by H. Gate in Wood
Lane about 300 yards beyond   N.B.—Bring this card with
Wood Lane Station Entrance.   you to secure admission.

The Mayoress's
Entertainment for the
22nd Battalion at the
White City. (B)

The Mayoress held a great concert in honour of the Battalion on 14th October. It was a typically 'Variety' mixture of patriotic songs, comedy sketches, short lectures, duets and so on, but the highlight was the beautiful Phyllis Dare singing (with its composer, her fiancé Kensington-born Paul Rubens, at the piano) the famous recruiting song 'Your King and Country want you' – the one with *We don't want to lose you, but we think you ought to go*, including a special adaptation of the words:

*We shall cheer you, thank you, **kiss** you*
When you come home again.

The *Kensington News* commented:

The song was received with tremendous enthusiasm, the audience joining wholehearted in the chorus. Miss Dare was recalled several times, and her efforts were heartily applauded.[29]

Many men who were there and survived the war remarked wistfully that they never did get the kisses!

On the other hand, conditions for training men and creating *esprit de corps* were not ideal in and around the White City, where there were now up to 20,000 men from all sorts of different units. Mayor Davison suggested to General Lloyd that the Battalion ought to move to winter quarters, and mentioned that its Commanding Officer, Lieutenant Colonel Innes, owned some suitable land at a place called Roffey, just north of Horsham, in Sussex. The General replied that if he wanted to move them that it had to be done at once. Things were hurriedly put in motion and the Battalion left from Addison Road Station on the morning of 27th October. Because of the rush, they were billeted in people's houses until such time as their new camp should be built.

Having moved the men, and having signed a building contract for the new camp, Mayor Davison might have thought he could get on with his other work, but:

A schedule of 10 closely printed pages reached me from the War Office, requiring me to provide in the course of a few weeks every kind of household requisite needed for a camp of 1,100 men, at a time when the Government had already bought up all available stock.[30]

1/13th Kensingtons officers. In the second row Captain CC Dickens is 6th left. In the front row, from fourth left we have: Major HH Campbell, Major HJ Stafford, Lt-Col LG Lewis, Captain Gilbert Thompson, Rev SE Pennefather and next (ie second right) Captain A Prismall. Lt-Col REF Shaw is the inset officer. (TK)

Boy Scouts made themselves useful in London by taking soldiers' kit to stations. (CHW)

These included beds, chairs, weighing machines, equipment for ablution rooms and shovels – right down to chess and backgammon sets. Even with the help of the excellent Mr Hames, his Private Secretary, this was a huge undertaking. He would get in trouble with the War Office for providing beds too high in quality (proper iron bedsteads with sprung mattresses) but he wanted his men to be as comfortable as possible.

At around the same time, the 1/13th Kensingtons were making last minute plans to go to France and on 3rd November, in front of the whole village, including all the schoolchildren, they moved down to Southampton to catch HMS *Matheran* to take the journey across the Channel to Le Havre. The whole embarkation went smoothly, with just one unexpected snag:

> *Considerable amusement was caused by the efforts of men trying to walk on the iron deck in nailed boots, they usually completing their journeys seated.* [31]

The voyage was uneventful and they took a train up to the St Omer area, where they remained for some days. They were almost at full strength (29 officers and 835 men). Some had not signed up for foreign service, while others were too young or too old and had to be left behind with the 2/13th Kensingtons. The latter were now being spoken of in the newspapers as a 'Home Battalion', although in time there would be a 3/13th reserve battalion that would train and send out drafts for the first two. In fact the 2/13ths would have quite a different set of adventures abroad. A number of other units abandoned the White City at this time, enabling the 2/13ths to move in there as a battalion rather than as a collection of 'day boys'.

Earlier, on 22nd September (after appropriate advance warning, telling the general populace not to fire on it), HMS Airship *Beta* had flown low over Kensington to great interest from those below, before heading off east in the direction of St Paul's Cathedral. Perhaps its voyage did instill some confidence that we could defend ourselves against the Zeppelin menace (the latter had already dropped bombs on

HMS Airship Beta; *quite impressive if one hadn't been exposed to a Zeppelin.*

Antwerp). Yet in the next month there was a run on 'Zeppelin Insurance' (damage from them was not covered by ordinary home insurance) and the lights in London were dimmed. As the days became shorter, accidents on the road (and even between pedestrians on the pavements) increased, and small businesses, such as retail tobacconists, began to suffer losses as few people shopped now in the later part of the evenings.

The great circling advance of the German Army through Belgium and parts of France had been stopped and a long line of trenches existed almost from Switzerland to the sea. It was trench war now, with British troops occupying small sectors in the north. The 1/13th Kensingtons moved forward from St Omer towards the front line and became part of 25 Brigade of 8th Division. On 18th November half of them (A and B Companies) relieved the 2nd Royal Berks in front line trenches near Fauquissart (not far east of Estaires, where the rest of the battalion was billeted). The trenches were in a dreadful water-logged condition, fifteen inches deep in some parts, and the weather was very cold. This was a moderately quiet sector – few attacks but a lot of sniping. For a new unit, for whom trench warfare had not been a great part of their training, they were going to have to learn from bitter experience how to keep safe from sniping: in the first few days they lost one man killed and four wounded. After three days A and B Companies exchanged places with C and D Companies and they would do this exchange for

Trenches in the Fauquissart/Laventie area in late 1914. (TK)

The Kensingtons at Fauquissart 1914' (F Percival) from the Architect and Contract Reporter. *(B)*

the next few months. The war diarist commented 'many men suffer from frostbite' – one thinks of Shackleton's polar expedition – but there was up to 17 degrees of frost and very little shelter. After he had come out of the trenches for the first time, Phil Ham wrote to his dad:

> *Our first experience, to say the least, wasn't pleasant. We not only had to contend with bullets, but extreme cold, which practically prevented even a few minutes sleep even in day time. We arrived back after three days rather the worse for wear, as you can imagine a trench isn't an ideal place for a week-end.[32]*

Later, when Sergeant HJ Stiles was blown up by a shell, he was wearing just about everything he owned:

> *The doctor in the field cut through my overcoat, tunic, cardigan, two shirts, my vest, I expect he wondered when he was coming to me.[33]*

Major Campbell appears to have been the first officer casualty in the 1/13th Kensingtons. He was wounded in the leg on 27th November

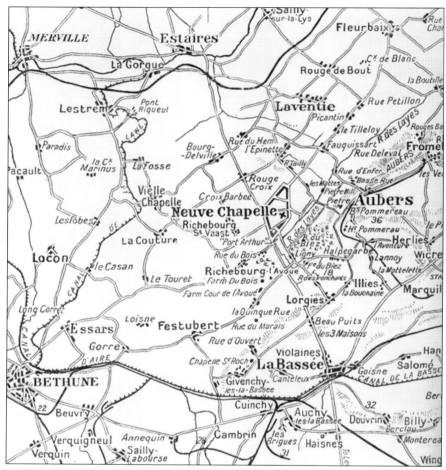

Where 1/13th Kensingtons served in 1914-15 (Fauquissart is between Laventie and Aubers). (THW)

and taken off to one of the base hospitals in France, where he was visited (presumably to his great surprise) by the king, who gave him a 'handsome walking stick' to help with his convalescence.

The dashing Captain Alan Burgoyne, MP for North Kensington, had been one of the very first to volunteer for the Colours. His regiment, the 4th King's Liverpool Regiment, an Extra-Reserve Battalion, was a hundred men short of achieving its establishment, so he came back to North Kensington and set up a meeting.

He stood before them that night not as their Member, but as a simple captain of infantry, and he appealed to them to come forward and act the part as simple privates in the infantry.

Two weeks later, by the sheer force of his personality, he took away with him 116 recruits on the train north.[34]

Horbury Church had turned its nearby Horbury Rooms into a home for maimed and homeless Belgian soldiers:

Captain Alan Burgoyne. (B)

> *Bright, capable and energetic helpers bustle about the rooms to attend to the wants of the occupants, for the poor soldiers themselves are worthy of every attention....They are being provided with the necessities of life through the generosity of Horbury Church and many other friends, but much remains to be done for them. You have nobly given someone or something for your country, and now there are these men in our midst. Will you help to provide their simple requirements?[35]*

Despite the war, Kensington still expected to see a large number of seasonal visitors from the dominions, particularly those emigrants from Britain that had made good and liked to 'do Christmas in the Old Country'. Others, of course, would be relatives of members of the armed forces of the dominions who were over here, while a third group would be those curious as to what conditions in war-torn London would be like.[36]

The Mayor asked the 1/13th what the best seasonal gifts for his men would be. The Quartermaster said wooden pipes or dark chocolate. In fact briar pipes went to the Kensington Fusiliers, but the 1/13th were given half a pound of chocolate per man as it was known by then that Princess Mary was sending a Christmas box, including pipes, to all men and women in uniform abroad.

The numbers of Belgian refugees was increasing and both boroughs were under pressure to find more homes for them. For those already here, the Mayor held a St Nicholas' Day fete for 500 children, mainly from Belgium. Some 2,000 toys were given out, plus entertainments

The refugees (at 'Kensington Guardians Institute' according to the New York Times *Pictorial Extra – but probably the Workhouse) look as though they have just been dumped here, until people can work out what to do with them.*

and refreshments, while the children of the Special Constables of Notting Hill Police Station organised 'at home' days for the wounded Belgian soldiers there, to entertain Belgian children in the Borough, with a fourteen foot Christmas tree with one or two gifts for all and feasts on the afternoons of January 1st and 2nd.[37]

The *Kensington News* in its Christmas Day editorial remarked on how inappropriate the traditional 'Peace on earth, goodwill to all men' message seemed, with so much of the world at war. The soldiers of the 1/13th Kensingtons might be thought the most luckless of all, in their trenches deep in water, yet the Christmas period would be a most memorable one for them.

It started on Christmas Eve. One officer described moving into the trenches then:

> *Shortly after settling in we heard a voice "Englishman, Englishman. Happy Christmas to you." And in answer "Same*

In Kensal Green (St Mary's Roman Catholic Cemetery) is this memorial to Belgian soldiers wounded in combat (mainly 1914 and early 1915), who had been evacuated to Britain but subsequently died here. (A)

to you and many of them." Soon Christmas trees all lighted up appeared in the German parapet and they started singing carols to which we replied. Later we heard there was to be no firing until 5 p.m. on Christmas Day. Next day after [early morning] stand-down we saw Germans walking about no man's land *in groups, and as I saw some of our men out too and also the men of the Scots Guards on our left, I allowed my men to go in pairs...The truce lasted all day and from the fraternisation we identified the enemy as the 13.126.158 German Infantry.*[38]

Many accounts have the meetings in no man's land being generated by a German crawling close to the British lines; thus Drummer Forrest wrote:

At last a voice was heard wishing us a Merry Xmas. Then one German crawled within 30 yards of our trenches and said that he had lived in England eight years and his wife and family still lived there, and said he desired no better country....He said, would one of us meet him half-way, so one of the —— got out and met him and came back with a bottle of whiskey and some cigars and the message "That if we did not fire they would not!" Well, this was agreed to, and next morning found both sides out of their trenches and mixing together and exchanging souvenirs.[39]

We had the very rare event of those lucky enough to be out of the line for Christmas Day visiting it as a tourist attraction:

We are now billeted in a racing stable at – [Laventie] *which is nearer to the trenches. Now I come to Christmas Day. We got out at seven o'clock, coffee and rum, went for a stroll, and returned for breakfast at eight. Steak, bacon, chips, bread, butter and jam. Strolled to the trenches and found all the men roaming around on the top. We walked half-way over and met the Germans, who had a long talk with us. Most of the men in front of us are London Germans with families in England. After exchanging cigarettes, cigars etc, strolled back again for dinner.*[40]

4th Corps' Christmas Card for 1914. Designs would get a lot better! (B)

Meanwhile the 2/13th Kensingtons had been spending much of their time being entrained and moved over to Essex to dig trenches for coastal defence in wet conditions almost as bad as for their sister battalion in France, but with no enemy opposite. This seemed rather less pointless in December after German cruisers shelled Hartlepool, West Hartlepool, Scarborough and Whitby (137 killed, 542 injured). Christmas leave was cancelled amid fears of invasion. Even so, they too had a memorable Christmas Day:

By arrangement the [regimental] *band had risen and paraded very early on Christmas morning, and whilst it was still dark outside, the lights were switched on, and shone down upon the hundreds of sleeping Kensingtons, who awoke to hear the strains*

The New Year attraction at the Empire - appropriately patriotic! (KN)

of "Christians, Awake!" sweeping gently through the great halls, softly at first, but swelling louder and louder. The bewildered men sat up in their beds, rubbing their eyes and wondering where they were. No one who was present on that occasion can ever forget the almost painful sweetness of the first moments, when the soft strains of that well-known tune stole upon their wakening consciousness.[41]

The Kensington Fusiliers, on the other hand, were having fun down in Horsham, being billeted in private houses for the most part, and forming friendships that would last the rest of their lives. Their popularity with the locals was greatly enhanced by the entertainers within the Battalion, with the *West Sussex Gazette* commenting in December:

> *It is only necessary now in Horsham to announce that the Royal Fusiliers are giving a concert to ensure the hall being filled to its uttermost limits.*

The showstopper almost every time was Private Teddy Rutland (Rutherford), with his 'ridiculous song, "I do like a nice mince pie!" and the singing lessons to the audience which accompanied it.'[42]

At the New Year's Eve Watch Night service at St Mary Abbots Church the 'immense' congregation waited for the Vicar of Kensington, Reverend Prebendary Pennefather, to summarise the year just gone. It may have surprised a few of them:

> *I don't suppose any of us are sorry to say good-bye to this year. It has been too sad and too eventful for us to mourn its departure. It was sad and eventful before this ghastly War broke out, when we were threatened by Civil War in our own Isles, and everything appeared to be going wrong with this country. God found for us a way out of many difficulties, and amidst the awful sorrows of this War, at any rate, we can thank God it has pulled us together; it has made all party strife and faction cease, and welded the different parts of the Empire together in a way no one ever expected.*[43]

CHAPTER 2

1915

*It was as if Daniel had invited the lion
to his den*

January was a dramatic time for the Mayors of Hammersmith and Kensington. First Mayor Foreman fell seriously ill with appendicitis, then Mayor Davison's wife's father, Sir Owen Roberts, died. On the other hand the Mayoress had been recently delivered of a son, who inevitably was called William Kensington Davison, and his christening was an august affair, sponsored by Princess Louise and the commanding officers of the 2/13th Kensingtons (Colonel McLean) and 22nd Royal Fusiliers (Colonel Innes), and carried out in front of a long list of aldermen and councillors. The infant appeared to enjoy his moment in the spotlight:

> *When in the arms of her Royal Highness the child seemed to be most contented, and on being handed to the aldermanic vicar* [Reverend Pennefather] *and named by the Princess, accepted the baptismal sprinkle with a happy smile both for Her Royal Highness and the Prebendary.*[44]

J Lyons of Cadby Hall appeared to have the exclusive catering contract for the Territorials at the White City. In early 1915 the company was summonsed and later convicted for supplying bad meat and for short-weight loaves. It is a comment on the times, however, that J Lyons were only fined £50 with £70 costs for their bad meat – meat that could have affected the health of thousands of men – whereas a young woman

*National Reservists took over some large dwellings in Cromwell Gardens as barracks. We have: 1) attestation 2) the drum and fife band 3) changing of the guard and 4) kit inspection. (*Daily Graphic*)*

Officers of the 2/13th Kensingtons. Centre of the second row Colonel McLean and on extreme right of this row is Captain JEL Higgins who transferred over to the 1/13th and would greet Mayor Davison on his visit to France in February 1916. (IWN)

The West London Coster and Street Trader Institute celebrated its first year of existence in January 1915 at its headquarters in Portobello Road. (B)

foolish enough to steal a petticoat from a pawnbroker's shop a few days after Christmas, right under the eyes of a watching policeman, was given one month's hard labour.

The 2/13th Kensingtons left Kensington for training in Maidstone in mid-January 1915. Whether the J Lyons cases had anything to do with their decision or not is not known but when they briefly returned to the Borough a few weeks later, they were billeted in private houses, not in the White City, before going first to Leatherhead and then Watford at the end of April to join their new division, the 60th.

The 3/13th Kensingtons had been able to drill in the grounds of Holland House, but now the owner, the Dowager Countess of Ilchester, decided to give the land over in preparation for the Royal Horticultural Show. Fortunately the patriotic Princess Louise stepped in to offer the large field (rented by Sir Robert Perks) north of Kensington Palace. More important for some of the troops was that the YMCA hut also had to be removed (a place was eventually found for it in the High Street).

Eventually space was found in waste ground on the High Street for another YMCA Hut. (THW)

The first major raid from the air was on 19th January on Great Yarmouth and King's Lynn: two killed in each place and sixteen injured. These places were on the coast; surely the Germans would not dare to bomb London?

The shortage of men already meant women could now be seen working in banks and municipal offices; they also served in provision shops, which had hitherto been a male preserve. This was in preference to being in service; many of Kensington's richer ladies agreed (and really meant it this time) that one just could not get servants these days.

A growing number of women produced a variety of articles from bandages and swabs to clothing, crutches and bedside tables in the new Kensington War Hospital Supply Depot at Kensington Square. This started 'with a capital of three five-pound notes and a staff of four energetic persons' and by the end of August would be operating from six locations in the Borough.[45]

Women from the newly formed Women's Volunteer Police Force were spotted in the West London Police Court taking notes, and the magistrate permitted them – as they were now professionals – to be

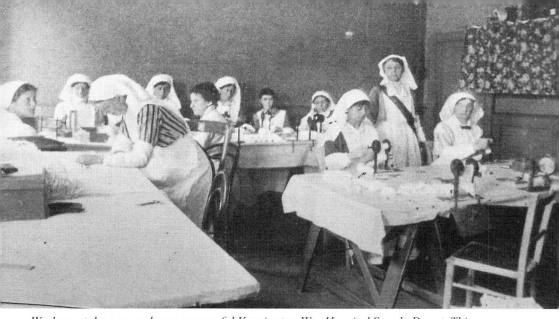

Workers at the new and very successful Kensington War Hospital Supply Depot. This is the roller bandage room. (B)

They also made casts. (B)

And papier-mâché boots, arm-cradles and splints. (B)

present for the sorts of cases from which women were normally banned.

Some women were, however, taking on some less socially desirable occupations; one local court report of a 'Woman charged with house-breaking' followed another of 'A female swindler sentenced'; while there was the story of the (suspicious, drunken) wife arrested for abusing the lady barber who shaved her husband.[46]

Reading reports about the Kensington Poor Law Guardians, one gets the impression that they saw job satisfaction more in terms of saving money rather than in the caring function. Thus after a long debate about how the wages of scrubbers, at 4d per hour (giving weekly wages of just 10/6d), were well below those in other boroughs, the Kensington Guardians passed a new rate of 5d per hour – only for the Finance Committee to then try and stop it, arguing that they should get 4½d at most. One way of reducing costs had been to recommend inmates to emigrate, but there were no takers in 1914. Now Hammersmith Guardians (seemingly more liberal) had come up with the revolutionary new idea of actively helping inmates get jobs: aiding with the applications, recommending on their behalf and so on.

Even so, one might expect the inmates of such institutions to resent the 'bare minimum' approach to their welfare. Not necessarily so: Private J Tarpy, of the Yorks and Lancaster Regiment, received a present of a pair of socks. Inside the socks was a message from Albert Howell of the (Poor Law) Kensington School at Marlesford Lodge:

> My dear Tommy Atkins…When we were out for a walk the other day a gentleman gave us a penny each to buy some sweets, but we thought we would like to do what little we could for our brave soldiers, so we are sending these socks with our best wishes for your success, and hoping you will return safely home. We think of you every day, and remember you in our prayers. I must say that more than 100 boys who have passed through this Poor Law School and several of our fathers are now at the Front.[47]

The local Gas, Light and Coke Company had supplied a number of the soldiers to the 1/13th Kensingtons. Mr Defries of the Gas Sales Department had sent several parcels over to the men, for which they were of course very grateful and Platoon Sergeant FJ Nickolay was keen to tell him about life at the front. They had given up on the flooded trenches and moved back thirty yards to breastworks, which they first had to build:

> *Consisting of, I was going to say bags of sand, but they are really bags of mud and clay. The breast work is about 6 feet to 7 feet high and about 7 feet thick, so you can just imagine the work there was with our legs stuck in the clay, and such clay as I have never contended with before.*

But they had not escaped water: in fact, from their billets they had to splash through flooded sugar beet fields for three-quarters of an hour to get to the breastworks:

The patriotic Gas, Coke and Light Company, which had a large gasworks at the top of Ladbroke Grove (KN)

> *Of course, you understand that this is at night and one cannot see the man in front, but you can hear now and again a dull splash and a voice call out to give a hand as they slip and fall in various attitudes in the slush and mud.*[48]

Gas, Light and Coke Company delivery cart, circa 1910. (rbkc)

In these conditions sniping was the only way to take the fight to the enemy, sometimes with surprising results. The enemy, if in sporting mood, might sometimes signal back 'miss' or 'inner', while Private Will Ramsay wrote:

"Liveliness" at the Bush Empire.

LEW LAKE AND HIS COLOSSAL COMPANY
IN AN
UP-TO-DATE MUSICAL COMEDY.
ENTITLED

"A Daylight Robbery,"

FULL CHORUS OF
50
CHARMING VOICES.

SPECIALITY DANCES by
THE BUSTER BROWNS
and
THE FAIRFAX SIX.

BEAUTIFUL SHOW OF
EVENING GOWNS
and UNIFORMS.

DANCES AND DUETS by
HAMLIN & MACK.

E. D. NICHOLLS
as Dripping, an Interpreter.

BOB MORRIS
as Jerry, a Railway Porter.

LEW LAKE
another Railway Porter.

NEXT WEEK.

SHEPHERDS BUSH EMPIRE
6.30——————THEATRE——————9.0.
THE "COLISEUM" OF WEST LONDON.

The other night, or just when it was getting dark, one of the fellows in the trench next to us fired several rounds at a German sniper's loophole, and we heard the beggar shout, "Hi, 'Arf a mo', Stop that game." It seemed quite funny to hear it.[49]

Sometimes the enemy was deadly serious and the popular Adjutant of the Kensingtons, Captain Thompson, was sniped on February 24th:

Lew Lake, a February attraction at the Bush Empire. (KN)

First of all, let me tell you that we have lost our dear Captain Thompson of St Mary Abbot's Terrace. He was killed on Wednesday morning last. He was home on leave the same time I was. The men in the trenches properly broke down when they heard the news, he was so liked by all. I believe there is not a single man who would not have followed him anywhere.[50]

Eric Kennington was another one lost to the Battalion in early 1915. He would go on to produce the marvellous *The Kensingtons at Laventie* painting and become a war artist in both this and the next war.

More substantial action was not far away. The (Territorial) 1/13th Kensingtons and four Regular army

Captain Gilbert Thompson, the Adjutant. (B)

battalions made up 25 Brigade of 8th Division. On 10th March the British IV Corps and the Indian Corps attacked at Neuve Chapelle, where there was a salient, or bulge, into the British lines. IV Corps,

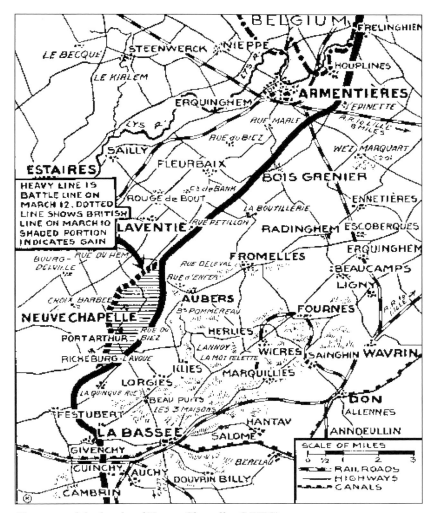

The area of the battle of Neuve Chapelle. (NYTC)

consisting of the 7th and 8th divisions, attacked towards the village
from the northwest, while the Indian Corps attacked from the west. 8th
Division attacked initially with 23 Brigade on the left and 25 Brigade
on the right. In turn, 25 Brigade attacked with 2nd Royal Berks and
2nd Lincolns, with 2nd Rifle Brigade and 1st Royal Irish Fusiliers in
support. Behind them, in reserve, were the 1/13th Kensingtons.

With the aid of a powerful bombardment, the British and Indian forces took Neuve Chapelle on 10th March, but were unable to exploit much further on the 11th. By this time the Germans had efficiently brought up lots of reserves, and on the 12th they attempted counter-attacks to regain the ground lost. Both the German and British/Indian attacks on the 12th were beaten back with heavy losses to the attackers. The net result was that the British and Indian forces managed to hold on to almost all of their first day gains, but it was again stalemate.

The Kensingtons did not have the glory of making an all-out assault on the Germans as a unit, but were heavily involved through supplying working parties and carrying up ammunition and barbed wire. They also helped prepare newly captured Neuve Chapelle for defence, and everyone had to face up to the intense German artillery fire. Even so, although the scale of their casualties was nothing like those in the attacking battalions (the Irish Rifles lost over 400 and the Lincolns over 300), they lost six officers and 150 other ranks. They had, however, created a favourable impression on their regular colleagues by their steadiness under fire, and there would be no surprise when they were named one of the attack battalions in the *next* battle.

Well-known casualties were Captain Eric Gates, son of Alderman Percy Gates, who had risen from private when the war started to captain; and Captain Arthur Prismall – at 53, a long-term local Volunteer and Territorial - whose son, Lieutenant MA Prismall, had just arrived with the Battalion as a replacement two days earlier.

Down in the Horsham area, mid-March also marked the time when the Fusiliers finally moved into the new huts in Roffey, about two miles outside the town. Now, with everyone collected together, the job of moulding the Battalion into a fighting unit could begin in earnest. Major Barker, the second in command, was responsible for more and more of the training, and he would be the

Major Barnett Barker, shortly to become Lieutenant-Colonel, who would take the 22nd Fusiliers to France and command them during almost all of their time there. (Sedburgh School)

The Mayor's Huts at Roffey just outside Horsham. (P-A)

man who would take the battalion to France, with Colonel Innes staying behind in charge of the new reserve battalion, the 27th Royal Fusiliers.

Easter holiday weather was dull – good for the Victoria & Albert Museum, which was busy – but there was still the traditional sight of nannies and nurses walking their children in Kensington Gardens. There they encountered young men (not in khaki) sailing their model boats and there was much comment about boys playing with toys when the nation needed volunteers.

Mr Fordham, the magistrate at the West London Police Court, was a man of forthright opinions who dispensed justice in an idiosyncratic and sometimes amusing manner. Thus in the case of the German alien

Neat and orderly displays in the Victoria & Albert Museum. (p-c, A)

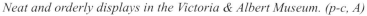

who was living with a woman not his wife – although he had claimed she was in his registration document – he announced that if the alien had been from a civilised country he would have reached a more severe judgment, but as he was from 'a barbarous country' where 'you have been brought up to believe that lying is a virtue', he discharged him.

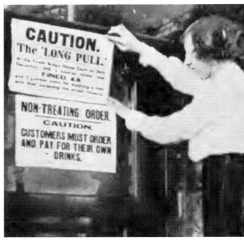

In the case of the drunken Belgian refugees he over-reached himself and caused a minor diplomatic incident. The problem was that there were lots of Belgian refugees, many of whom could not speak English, whose

The Non-Treating Order. (THW)

needs for food and shelter were being met, but not the need to regain self-respect by getting a job to earn money and provide for oneself and one's family. As a result they were bored and had little to do all day. Just occasionally they would be given some money and it was no surprise when some ended up being arrested for being drunk. This coincided with a lot of talk (Lloyd George and others) about the demon drink being more detrimental to the war effort than U-boats, with King George setting an example by signing the pledge to abstain from alcohol until the end of the war. 'Treating', ie groups drinking together where everyone buys a round, was denounced as the great evil.

On 3rd April there were six Belgian refugees in front of Mr Fordham for drunkenness, and he remarked that he could not understand why they were not fighting for their country. He was assured that it was Easter, a big festival in Belgium. He fined them ten shillings each and the fee of the interpreter.

The next week he had several Belgians charged with drunkenness and one of being drunk and disorderly. Mr Fordham said the latter looked to be a strong fellow that ought to be fighting for his country, and remarked; 'It looks like we have got the scum of Belgium here'. Scum and Belgium were two words that ought not to have been in the same sentence, and 'a highly-placed Belgian' wrote an angry letter to *The Times*, while Herbert Samuel, the President of the Local

Government Board, was also critical. In his following week's Court, this time having to deal with two Belgians accused of stealing from a third refugee, Mr Fordham was obliged to praise all things Belgian: 'no one had a greater appreciation of the Belgian nation than he'. No doubt someone had informed him of the presence in court of the Superintendent of the Earls Court Belgian Refugee Camp, who was 'very pleased to hear His Worship's remarks'.[51]

A few days after the Germans had used poison gas for the first time on the Western Front on 22nd April against French troops at Ypres, the War Office asked for respirators. As soon as the Red Cross office in Upper Phillimore Place opened at 10 am:

> *Every worker I am told, arrived with the same thought, that ordinary work must be laid aside for a day, in order to meet the sudden call. Out of many ideas, plus the official directions, a good pattern of respirator was evolved, and approved at the Army Ordnance Department, Pimlico.*

They had made some 200 by the end of the day and these were hurriedly passed on to the headquarters of the troops.[52]

Anger at the Germans for using asphyxiating gas was greatly amplified when the news of the sinking of the *Lusitania* on 7th May came through (with the deaths of 1,198 people). One can understand the riots at the Broadway Cinema, North Kensington, which was featuring the *Lusitania* incident, when two Germans 'expressed their satisfaction with the occurrence', for which they were 'most properly ejected and mauled'; but gangs then went around damaging shop fronts of 'enemy aliens' from Kensal Town in the north of the Borough right down to Fulham, beyond the Borough boundaries in the south. The great shame was that it was undiscriminating and included many who were naturalised, like Mr E Wittekind, owner of the popular baker's shop

Two 'frightful' incidents one after the other generated enormous anger. (p-c, A)

This is 'somewhere in London', but the scene was repeated almost everywhere. (Peel, How)

in Uxbridge Street, whose family had been here since Victorian times. Mr Wittekind protested that he had a son in the British Army and another in the British Navy. The local Special Constables showed great bravery in trying to stop the crowds running amok and in attempting to restore order.

On 9th May the 1/13th Kensingtons got the chance to win their spurs. At what would become known as the Battle of Aubers Ridge, they were given an important role to play at the extreme left of the British line of advance. They were to go forward, take some German trenches, stop short of the enemy strongpoint at Delangre Farm, wheel left and make a defensive flank to protect the advanced British troops against counter-attacks from the left.

The opening bombardment was by no means as strong as that at Neuve Chapelle (too few and overused guns, along with very poor quality ammunition), but in their favour were two mines blown in the German lines at zero hour (5.40 am). They advanced either side of the right-hand crater and were able to find gaps in the German wire and, with difficulty and suffering considerable casualties – probably from the strongpoint in front of them, Delangre Farm, which seemed to have been untouched by British artillery – managed to move through the

German trenches. Another costly effort was involved before they could create the defensive line on the left, but within an hour and a half they had achieved all their objectives.

Yet there was no one on either side of them; they were completely in the air. The British attack, anticipated by an alert and well-organised enemy, had been driven back with heavy losses in most places. The Royal Irish on the right of the Kensingtons had great difficulty getting forward of their trenches in the area next to the Kensingtons; and so too the battalion following behind them, the 2nd Lincolns. Now no man's land was a death trap because of enemy artillery and machine guns: of thirty German prisoners sent back through no man's land towards the British lines, only ten actually made it there alive.

The Kensingtons' War Diary is full of piteous unanswered requests for men and ammunition, and messages detailing the whittling down of their numbers and the gradual encroachment of the enemy, before Brigadier General Pinney ordered them to withdraw to the British lines at 2.45 pm. This retreat was said to be the most costly part of the whole exercise, the survivors having to fight their way back through the German trenches and make their way the best they could across the deadly no man's land.

Private Craig survived, but the retreat did for many of his pals:

After a long day of rapid fire, and standing up to one's armpits in mud and water, we had the order to retire; that was when we lost our men; out of my bombing party there were two left, I [sic] included.

The Germans seemed to mass up in thousands as we retired, and the rifle fire was awful. We were all cut with barbed wire, and by the time I got to our own trenches I had lost everything...

Fred is still alive. There was him, an officer and 30 men started to come back, but only Fred and the officer arrived. I myself received a bullet through my haversack, but their dum-dums don't seem to like me.[53]

Initially only about fifty-five men got back but others dribbled in after dark. Their total casualties were thirteen officers and 423 other ranks out of twenty-one officers and 602 other ranks before the battle: a 70 per cent loss rate. For the time being the Battalion was finished as a fighting force, and in fact left the 8th Division shortly afterwards to become lines of communications troops guarding railway lines, loading/offloading wagons and so on. It would stay on these duties until February 1916, when, reinforced once more, it joined 56th Division and began life anew as fighting troops.

It took quite some time for the news to get back to Kensington that there had been a battle, and how serious it was:

> *When the news filtered through some few days ago that the fight on the 9th inst had been costly, not to say disastrous, to the local corps, there were many anxious inquirers at* [Kensington Territorial] *headquarters, and the stream has continued each day since. The publication on Monday of the list of nine officers killed opened one's eyes to the probable extent of the total casualties, and gradually the truth leaked out. Expressions of regret are heard on all sides. These men formed the pick of our citizen soldiers, and the brief accounts that have come through from the survivors prove that a very gallant stand was made against the hordes of Germans who were sent against them.*[54]

Mayor Davison wrote immediately to the Battalion's CO, Colonel Lewis:

> *Dear Colonel Lewis, The people of Kensington are deeply grieved to hear of the heavy price in officers and men which our regiment has sustained in the fighting of the last few days. Please let the officers and men who are left know how proud we are of the splendid gallantry they have shown on every occasion since they have been in France. They have indeed won a name for themselves and added a lustre to Kensington which will never be forgotten.*
>
> *Believe me, very truly yours, MAYOR.*
>
> *PS My Fusilier Battalion (the 22nd Royal Fusiliers) are straining at the leash to go out and give your fellows a helping hand.*

Major Stafford (as Colonel Lewis was in hospital) replied, in best Simonides of Ceos style:

Please tell the people of Kensington that the Battalion, which has the honour to bear the name of the Royal Borough, has done its duty, and has since it has been serving here never failed to carry out what is required to do. He added, *We have lost many comrades, and our numbers are much reduced; we shall continue, as long as there are any of us left, to do our duty and maintain the name of Kensington.*[55]

In fact Acting-Sergeant FW Shepherd was determined to add 'a lustre' all by himself. He had won the DCM for gallant conduct on several occasions back in November–December 1914, including rescuing a wounded man while under fire. He now became one of only six men in the Army at this stage in the war to win a clasp to the medal:

On May 9th, during the operation near Rouge Bancs, he made his way from the firing line for over 400 yards to the enemy's breastworks with a telephone line. Before he reached his destination the line was cut. He crawled on to the Signal Section, and started laying another line, which eventually got through. He was under a heavy fire the whole time: fourteen men had already been killed and wounded passing over the same ground. He subsequently carried two wounded men to a place of safety under a heavy fire. His conduct throughout the action was magnificent.[56]

Many Kensington families had no idea whether their 'missing' son (or husband or father) was alive or dead, but by early June Private Croft's parents had received a letter from him at the Rennbahn Prisoner of War

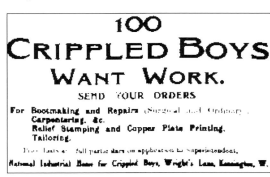

Five of their boys had managed to join the forces (the Home was for neglected and ill-used boys as well as those permanently crippled). They had a pleasant surprise in January when they received Prince George's 30-pound birthday cake – big enough for a decent piece for all 100 inmates. (KN)

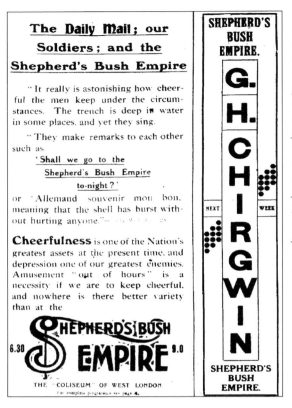

The Daily Mail; our Soldiers; and the Shepherd's Bush Empire

" It really is astonishing how cheerful the men keep under the circumstances. The trench is deep in water in some places, and yet they sing.

" They make remarks to each other such as

'Shall we go to the Shepherd's Bush Empire to-night ?'

or 'Allemand souvenir mon bon, meaning that the shell has burst without hurting anyone."

Cheerfulness is one of the Nation's greatest assets at the present time, and depression one of our greatest enemies. Amusement "out of hours" is a necessity if we are to keep cheerful, and nowhere is there better variety than at the

SHEPHERD'S BUSH EMPIRE
6.30   9.0
THE "COLISEUM" OF WEST LONDON

SHEPHERD'S BUSH EMPIRE.

G. H. CHIRGWIN

NEXT   WEEK

SHEPHERD'S BUSH EMPIRE.

The Shepherd's Bush Empire and Cheerfulness. GH Chirgwin was normally partly blacked-up with a white diamond over one eye as the 'White-faced Kaffir'. He was a variety evening all of his own: playing the Japanese one-stringed fiddle, dancing while playing the bagpipes and the crowd's favourite, singing the tear-jerker 'The Blind Boy'. (KN)

Camp, Munster, Westphalia, saying that he was being well treated, and later Private Albert Gretener furnished the names of seventeen 13th Kensingtons men who were being held there.

In April the Shepherd's Bush Empire found itself mentioned in the *Daily Mail* in a piece about the morale of troops. The astute marketing men at the Bush Empire soon used it in an advertisement on the theme of 'cheerfulness' – best maintained by regular visits to the variety at the Bush Empire.[57]

The Mayor's Fusilier battalion moved at the end of June from Horsham to Clipstone Camp (near Mansfield) for brigade and divisional training; they were in 99 Brigade of 33rd Division, all New Army units. Compared to their comfortable Roffey huts, this place was only half-finished, but after a week or so of hard labouring, it was almost fit for occupation. There was a major snag, however:

Oh! Roffey Camp, we miss you!
Our hearts are sad and sore;
Your canteen charged 2d per pint,
But here it's a penny more.[58]

They would stay there just a month before travelling down to Tidworth (Salisbury Plain) for divisional manoeuvres. RSM McCausland had been finally persuaded to accept a commission and he would go to France as Captain McCausland, commander of C Company. On 1st July the Mayor's direct responsibility for the Battalion came to an end, but the War Office's letter of thanks and acknowledgements to him contained a sting in the tail in the last sentence:

> *I am to add that its success on active service will largely depend on the results of your efforts to keep the depot companies constantly up to establishment with men in every way fit for service.*[59]

There was a very public furore about the setbacks the British Army had suffered in March and May. Patently one of the causes was the lack of shells and guns: the guns that were present were overworked (which creates inaccuracy), while there was a total shortage of ammunition, especially the high-explosive variety, and much of that was dud. One of the more immediate responses was be the creation of the Ministry of Munitions under Lloyd George – just the man to galvanise the whole process.

The Zeppelin: rather larger and more potent than our own airships. (NYTC)

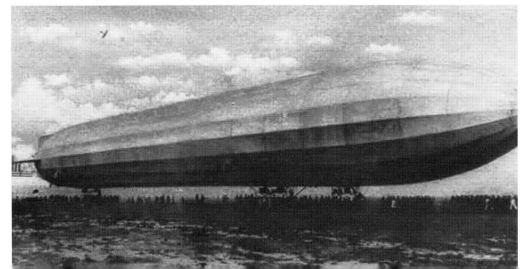

The first Zeppelin raid on London occurred on 31st May – fortunately for Kensington, the raider, L38, dropped his bombs and incendiaries in north-east London in places like Stoke Newington and Dalston. Compared to HMS *Beta*, that flew over Kensington in 1914, the Zeppelins were huge and scary objects, so when news came through that Sub-Lieutenant RAJ Warneford had managed to fly above a returning Zeppelin near Ghent and destroy it by dropping bombs on it, the feat absolutely captured public imagination – not least the king, who immediately awarded Warneford the Victoria Cross. More information became available, making it an even more heroic feat: he had to dodge machine-gun fire from the Zeppelin before he could get above it; his first five bombs failed and it was only the last one that did

Sub-Lt RAJ Warneford, who became everyone's hero. (THW)

Artist's imagining of Warneford bringing down the Zeppelin. The explosion did turn his plane upside down, and stopped his propeller. (WI)

the trick, with the resultant explosion stopping his plane's engine, meaning he had to come down and land behind enemy lines. Foreshadowing the fictional war hero, Biggles, he then spent thirty-five minutes on the ground repairing his machine before flying off home.

Unfortunately the airman was killed in a simple flying accident a few days later. Because of the great public interest, Warneford's body was brought back from France, where large crowds reverently awaited

Taking Warneford's coffin to its interment at Brompton Cemetery. (WI)

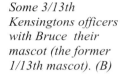

Some 3/13th Kensingtons officers with Bruce their mascot (the former 1/13th mascot). (B)

the late night arrival of the coffin at Victoria Station. A guard of honour from the Royal Naval Division then took it to repose overnight in the chapel at Brompton Cemetery. The next day people started arriving four hours before the ceremony, and so filled the cemetery that its gates had to be locked, with thousands of late-comers filling the streets outside.

There was a continual need for recruits for the 13th Kensingtons, particularly for the 2/13th, which had been supplying large drafts to boost the tiny numbers of the 1/13th, and for the 3/13th (now in Richmond Park) which would probably just do home service. Other nearby Boroughs had opted for Artillery: Fulham was onto its third Royal Field Artillery Brigade, while a Heavy Battery and Ammunition

*The 2/13th
Kensingtons on
manoeuvres.
(IWN)*

Column, plus a Divisional Ammunition Column was in the process of being raised by Mayor Foreman in Hammersmith.

Yet by the summer of 1915 recruiting had become very sluggish and the National Registration Act was passed on 15th July to find out exactly how many men (and women) of military age (recently raised to 40) there were, and their details of employment, so that the authorities could accurately estimate the pool of potential recruits, minus those who worked in key industries. This was a major data collecting and data analysing exercise, and the results would not be known until the autumn. Meanwhile, any likely young man strolling down the street not wearing uniform was likely to have a white feather thrust at him. In some cases this would have unforeseeable circumstances:

> *The remarks of Mr Reginald Kemp J.P., deputy coroner for West Middlesex, in the course of an inquest on a Shepherd's Bush taxi-driver* [Richard Charles Roberts] *who, rejected from the Army for a weak heart, was driven to suicide by the taunts of women and amateur recruiters, emphasise the growth of a nuisance Mr Kemp not inaptly described as scandalous.*[60]

There was also an immense need for workers in the munitions industry. Women represented a major resource that had been barely tapped (unlike in France and Germany), but the relevant unions were more concerned about 'dilution' – women being used as cheap labour – while some conservative manufacturers were hard to persuade that women *could* make a useful contribution in their industry. Lloyd George would have a battle on his hands to introduce women against such opposition, but it would help if there was seen to be strong demand from women themselves. The WSPU (the suffragettes) had switched from being outside the law before the war to enthusiastic supporters of the war effort, wanting to do more. One can almost see his brain working out a devilish scheme.

On July 17th some 30,000 women marched through western and central London in pouring rain to demand their 'right to serve'. The procession was made even more moving and memorable through its inclusion of a 'Pageant of the Allies', headed by a young woman dressed in Grecian white with gold trimming, bearing the flags of the allied countries. Behind her, pride of place was given to Belgium:

The soul of that martyred but unconquerable land was vividly typified by a tall, slender lady dressed in mourning, with a purple veil bound round her head and flowing in a long streamer behind. She carried aloft the flag of her country, torn and tattered but still beautiful in its colours of black, yellow and red. She walked barefoot through the slush of the roadways – heavy rain having fallen earlier – and on her delicately chiselled face there was an expression of pride and sorrow and devotion, all of a high degree.

In contrast, France 'walked with a swagger in her *tricoleur* frock and red cap of liberty, and charmed the spectators with her merry smile.'[61]

A 'visibly moved' Lloyd George then received a deputation headed by his former bête noir, Mrs Pankhurst (who claimed to be involved in

The

WOMEN'S
GREAT PROCESSION.

We are faced by the danger of losing our freedom as a Nation. If the country is to be saved women must be allowed to help. The service that they can render is enough to make the difference between defeat and victory in this war. On Saturday afternoon, July 17th, Mr. Lloyd George will receive a deputation and hear women's demand for the right to make munitions and render other war service.

Before the deputation is received a great procession will march through the West End of London in order to impress the world with the fact that British women are ready and determined to give their help to Britain in her hour of need.

You can help. The first thing to do is to

Join the Great Procession of
WILLING WOMEN WORKERS on

SATURDAY, JULY 17

The procession will form up on the Victoria Embankment at 2.30 p.m. and start promptly at 3.30.

Fill in this form and send it to-day to the Secretary, W.S.P.U. War Service, Lincoln's Inn House, Kingsway, W.C

——— WOMEN'S WAR SERVICE. ———

I intend to march in the War Service Procession forming up on the Victoria Embankment at 2.30 p.m., on Saturday, July 17.

Name..

Address ....

The recruitment poster for the Right to Serve march, organised by the WSPU, but underpinned by Ministry of Munitions money. (A)

A 'visibly moved' Lloyd George's addresses the procession. (THW)

'Belgium' with its tattered flag and indomitable nature. (THW)

Some of the marchers. No fear of being roughly handled by the police this time. (THW)

the 1913 burning of his Walton Heath house), at the Ministry of Munitions. Then he and the deputation went out to address the marchers waiting at Victoria Embankment. One marcher said:

It was a strange sight to see Mr Lloyd George fearlessly fraternising with Mrs Pankhurst; it was as if Daniel had invited the lion to his den. [62]

Here the interests of Lloyd George and Mrs Pankhurst coincided exactly and it was no coincidence that the Ministry of Munitions had quietly advanced £3,500 to Mrs Pankhurst's group to help with organising expenses. He 'gladly and eagerly' accepted their offers of help. He promised them the same rates for piece-work as men, and a proper minimum rate for time work, but cautioned them to be patient while he set things in motion.

The task of distributing and collecting the National Register forms for everyone aged between 15–65 in the Borough (blue for men, white for women) would be a straightforward task for the unpaid, volunteer helpers; except perhaps in Notting Dale, where, in the delicate language of the time:

A visitor is generally looked upon with some suspicion, and may receive a welcome warmer than is considered pleasant and: *That part of the Borough will, I believe, be delegated to remunerated and more seasoned workers.* [63]

Meanwhile it seemed that the National Amalgamated Union of Shop Assistants, Warehousemen and Clerks was finally going to help the Belgian refugees – many of whom were in the equivalent Belgian unions such as 'Unitas' – to acquire work, by defraying travel expenses, offering emergency accommodation and so on. The Belgians did have to ensure they did not accept work under the British union's minimum wage, of course; use of the Belgians as cheap labour had been the union's main fear.

There was another major visitation by Zeppelins on 8th September. The main areas targeted were well to the east of Kensington, but as Commander Mathy's L13 approached from the north-west before turning east, to drop most of its bombs from Russell Square to

What the Germans hoped for from their Zeppelin raids. (p-c, A)

Liverpool Street, it no doubt sounded a lot nearer. Although the death toll was just twenty-two, some of the incendiary bombs dropped created considerable damage to property in the Cripplegate area amounting to around half a million pounds: indeed it was said that the Germans had targeted the area after reading reports of a huge fire there in 1897 getting out of control.[64]

On October 19th Mr Miyatovitch spoke at Kensington Town Hall on 'The War and the Balkans'. He was a recognised master of his subject, but it was perhaps more interesting that this was one of a series of six talks on war issues organised by the South Kensington Branch of the London Society for Women's Suffrage, one of the oldest of the suffrage societies, which was formed from the Kensington Society in 1867, and was now part of the NUWSS, the suffragists. The latter had suspended their normal politicking in order to provide education, training and hostels (in contrast with the WSPU, the suffragettes, who had flipped from violent protest into full support for the war).

Mr Miyatovitch – the best known progressive Serbian in London.

Continuing on a Serbian theme, Vaso Marinkovitch, described as a showman, was charged with cruelly working a pony when it was lame, and with cruelty to a bear by causing it unnecessary suffering by exhaustion. The pony hauled the van, while the bear was chained by the nose and neck to its back axle. An RSPCA inspector saw the distress of the pony, then came across the emaciated bear, so exhausted that when the Inspector released it from the chains, it simply fell over. Van, bear and pony were taken to the police station, where they discovered the owner hiding in the van. All agreed that the pony was too far gone and ought to be put down, but the bear might survive if it was to receive considerable extra nourishment.

The Mayor was guest of honour at the Fusiliers Sergeants' Mess to celebrate a year since the founding of the Battalion (B)

Mr Fordham, the magistrate, could not restrain himself: 'Then the bear had better eat the pony'. He then enquired if the Zoological Gardens would take the bear. Unfortunately the Canadian armed forces had brought so many bears over to Britain as regimental mascots, which they had subsequently left with the zoo when they went away to fight, that it had quite enough bears for the moment. Mr Fordham then sentenced the Serb to one month's hard labour, with a recommendation for deportation.[65]

There was a further Zeppelin raid on 13th October, called the Theatreland Raid, as L15 dropped its first bombs on the Lyceum Theatre in Wellington Street (just off the Strand), one bomb in particular, exploding just outside the nearby Old Bell public house at a theatre interval, killing seventeen and injuring twenty people. In all forty-seven people were killed in the London area.[66]

Lord Derby's scheme for men voluntarily to attest their willingness now to join up later when their age and marital status group was due, did have some success. Some of the volunteers were not perhaps the ones expected:

THE
Royal Borough of Kensington.

ENLISTMENT in
H.M. FORCES.

The Council hereby give notice to all officers and men on the permanent staff who are of military age (other than those specially exempted) that they do not bind themselves to extend to such of them as may enlist after the 11th December, the privileges as regards pay and reinstatement which have been granted to men who have already joined H.M. Forces.

By Order,

WM. CHAMBERS LEETE,
Town Clerk.

Town Hall,
Kensington, W.
30th November 1915

As far as the Council was concerned, if you had to be forced into joining up, you forfeited the privileges they were offering. (B)

DARKENED STREETS

Now that enforced lighting restrictions are in operation, it is more than ever necessary to take great care in crossing the streets, and to make use of the refuges provided for people wishing to cross the road.

★   ★   ★

In crossing a street look out for approaching traffic from the right hand until the centre of the roadway is reached, then from the left hand. The straight way is the shortest way. Don't cross obliquely, especially at the intersection of two streets. It is also useful to remember that at recognised crossings police men are on duty. Cross at a street lamp so as to be seen.

★   ★   ★

When hailing a bus passengers should endeavour to stand under or as near as possible, to a street lamp, and give a direct signal to stop the bus by holding up the hand. This gives the motor-bus driver an opportunity of seeing a prospective passenger some yards in advance and bringing the bus to a stop safely and conveniently.

The London General Omnibus Co., Ltd.,
Electric Railway House,
Broadway, Westminster, S.W.

The dark streets were dangerous at night and the number of accidents went up sharply in 1915, (KN)

Apparently not able any longer to restrain his desire to "do his bit", a well-clad boy, evidently of parents of a superior class, walked into the Town Hall one day last week, and announced to the astonished recruiting officer that he wished to enlist under Lord Derby's scheme. The importance of it being Lord Derby's scheme was particularly emphasised. He gave his age as seven years three months. The officer at once appreciated the martial enthusiasm of the lad and took him in for a medical test. The ordinary procedure was observed, and proved satisfactory. The lad demanded an armlet [to prevent him getting a white feather], *and was told to call on a later date. Then his nurse, who had missed him from the street, put in an appearance, and escorted him home.*[67]

When the king himself made a personal appeal for more men to come forward, this was an indication that something was seriously wrong; it did feel as if a lot of men were still slipping through the net; 1916 would herald the introduction of conscription.

Captain Alan Burgoyne MP had switched to the 17th Middlesex (the Footballers Battalion, first raised at Fulham in December 1914, with Mayor Norris and the Fulham MP, Hayes Fisher, two of the prime movers), who left for France on 18th November. He was hugely impressed by the way the French people had embraced the idea of the whole nation at war:

National Registration Act card. (rbkc)

The French are amazing in their courage and their optimism. My hostess is an old widow, and she has lost a husband and two sons, a third is home wounded, and the last came on six days' leave yesterday, after six months bloody work. Every woman is in mourning – and France knows, every man, woman and child, what war means. 'Tis a fight of nations – slackers, stay-at-homes, and excuse-makers are unknown. I should add, however, having regard to the spirit of the men under me, that my own belief is that ignorance most largely controls the hanging back – ignorance. If they only knew and could see the results of war which this gallant nation accepts as a necessary sacrifice we should have three million men come forward tomorrow.[68]

Inside of the card (rbkc)

The 22nd Fusiliers arrived in France the day before the 17th Middlesex. Like the latter, they found themselves transferred into the 2nd Division – regulars, who had been 'out' since 1914. The 22nd stayed in 99 Brigade, along with the 23rd Royal Fusiliers (and welcomed the regular 1st KRRC and 1st Royal Berks), while other changes meant that the Division now had six raw New Army battalions and six Regular battalions.

In late November the 22nd Royal Fusiliers were gradually introduced to trench warfare at Cambrin, near La Bassée, first in small numbers sandwiched between larger numbers of regular soldiers, then in company-sized chunks holding limited stretches of line. If they but knew it, it was a gentler introduction to the trenches than the 1/13th Kensingtons had had last year, but the bad weather was similar, as Colonel Barker told his wife:

> *The men came back from the trenches today. Yesterday was warm and it poured all night; the thaw has done awful damage and the trenches were falling in all right. They were building [them] up with sandbags all the time. In spite of every precaution most of the rifles got choked up with dirt. The men were mud from head to foot and wet thoroughly up to their waists; I never saw such a forlorn lot. I had tea and rum with bacon, bread and jam waiting for them on return; their feet were all washed and massaged and then they turned to their breakfasts. I visited them all and found them most cheery and delighted. I love them all, they are splendid.*[69]

The Empire's offering for mid-November 1915. (KN)

It was soon time for the Mayor to be sending Christmas gifts to his Fusiliers: 1,030 boxes containing a cigarette holder and six cigarettes from himself, with 1,050 boxes of fifty cigarettes plus 1,050 half-pound tins of chocolate from the Mayoress and Friends in the Borough. As luck would have it, the 22nd were to be in the front line trenches on Christmas Day; would there be another 'Christmas Truce'? It was not to be: firstly officialdom forbade it; and then the weather ruled it out. Private Paul Destrubé, one of three Canadian brothers, told his girlfriend:

> *Christmas Eve it rained all night, and as a waterproof ground sheet does not offer ideal shelter, we did not spend the most pleasant of nights. However, the following day the sun beamed upon us, and under its drying and brightening influence life assumed a better aspect, and we broke into song and merriment.*[70]

In fact the 27th December, when they were out of the trenches, was designated their official Christmas Day when all their (remaining) parcels from home could be consumed.

Someone called Sigma – undoubtedly Christopher Stone, in charge of the Signallers – wrote a long and interesting account of the doings of the Mayor's Fusilier Battalion:

> *Our first experience in the trenches left us very dirty and tired – but of course as keen and undaunted as ever; and there is probably not a man in the battalion who would not rather have spent Christmas in the trenches than at Tidworth. It was an uneventful day on the whole, although heralded by considerable artillery activity on Christmas Eve, and I do not know how to convey to you at home the mixture of monotonous routine and of interesting episode that makes up the usual time in the trenches. The work on fatigue parties, clearing communication trenches knee-deep in mud; building up parapets and traverses that the wet weather had demolished; trudging back through miles of trench to fetch rations in sandbags or water in petrol cans; cleaning rifles all the time, on sentry-go hour on, hour off, trying to keep wet feet warm, boiling pannikins on charcoal*

braziers for the tea in the cold night watches, 'standing to' at dusk and dawn – all the details of the endless round of duties are very fatiguing to the normal year-trained man…

He went on:

…the amazing spirit of the men. You wouldn't believe it unless you saw it actually under your eyes. Cool, cheerful, laughing, grousing, covered with mud, drenched to the skin – they are the finest fellows in the world; every day a little more knowing and self-reliant, and able to extract comfort from apparently impossible situations and billets. They pick up things quickly! Kensington has every reason to be proud.

"MOTORING"

HARRY TATE

REYNOLDS & Co., BERNERS STREET, LONDON, W.1

Harry Tate's famous Motoring sketch was published by Reynolds & Co. (A)

After thanking Kensington for all its gifts to the men, he added:

But a good many letters are written every day that find their way to Kensington addresses, and no doubt most of your readers are well up in our experiences and feelings. But to the others, to all of them, I would just like to say this – that it would do your hearts real good if you could see out here in their daily life the men that you knew in Kensington in the days before the war. They are splendid.[71]

Alas, censorship had greatly changed in the British press over the last year, when there

Short & Sons of Notting Hill were possibly the premier specialist butcher in the Borough. This is their tempting special offer for New Year. (KN)

SHORT & SONS, LTD.

Special Offer,

One Week only.

Shoulders

OF

Southdown or Scotch

Mutton,

10½d.

per lb.

SHORT & SONS, LTD.,

15, 17, 19,

High Street, Notting Hill Gate.

might have been several letters from the front from the 1/13th Kensingtons in every edition.

In fact the sort of censorship that had been introduced was particularly irking the editor of the *Kensington News*. While stressing he had been adhering to the Press Bureau guidelines as to what might or might not be published, he felt these had been ridiculous with regards to air raids, as 'no peril is more terrifying than the unknown peril'. Not knowing led to exaggeration and panic. Even more important than the details of the air raids was their suppression altogether.

There had been a number of changes to the lives of Britons in the last year, leading to more state control and there would be even more in the next year. Meanwhile there was Harry Tate in his famous *Motoring* sketch on at the *Bush Empire* for Christmas Week.

CHAPTER 3

1916

Then mid-high in the now lurid glowing heavens
we behold the Zeppelin

In early January the 2/13th Kensingtons moved off to Warminster for final training with other units of the 60th Division before going overseas. They had a new CO: the fiery Lieutenant Colonel McLean, who had recruited them in 1914 and been with them ever since, was deemed too old to go abroad with his battalion and he was replaced by Lieutenant Colonel CM Mackenzie, a quietly impressive 1/13th officer who had returned from France.

The advertisements for the Shepherd's Bush Empire now came out with a new theme: 'The Bushman Family' (Bushman, Mrs Bushman, and Reggie and Dolly Bushman, their children), expressed as a strip cartoon around the edges of their display advertisement. That meant that they could still argue the case for happiness as a key weapon against war depression in the inside block, while evincing other less obvious benefits of the Bush Empire through the words of the Bushman Family, thus:

Dolly Bushman: We must bring Uncle-Sergeant Bill here next week, eh? Won't he be pleased to be home to see us? And won't he like the gramophone, Reg?

Reggie: Isn't it good of the Bush Empire to have a gramophone for us, and such nice seats in the waiting room? At other theatres they have to wait in the rain, don't they? Ha! Ha![72]

The introduction of the ultra-patriotic Mr Bushman and his family. (KN)

The war claimed another prominent Kensington man's son. The *Kensington News* found dignified words:

> *Everyone associated in public or private life with Mr W Chambers Leete, the honoured Town Clerk of Kensington, will be grieved by the calamity that has befallen him and Mrs Chambers Leete in the loss of their only son, Captain W.J.H. Leete, of the 11th Lancashire Fusiliers, killed in action on the 21st inst.*[73]

On 9th February a special meeting of Kensington Borough Council was held to discuss the composition of the new Military Service Act tribunals (to cover appeals against conscription). But what everyone wanted to hear about was

W Chambers Leete, the esteemed town Clerk. (B)

The Mayor and Mayoress inspecting a guard of honour of Boy Scouts at Portobello Road school. (B)

The Mayor's cross-channel reservation. (B)

Menu
Février 1916

Potage perlé
Sardines — Beurre de ...

Veau au jus
Purée de pommes dorée

Choux Fleurs gratinés

Gigot
Flageolets blancs

Fromages
Desserts
Crème au Moka
Biscuits des Alliés

Café

Special menu for the British VIP visitors. (B)

the Mayor's adventures in France. Mayor Davison had been one of eight people involved in recruiting who had been invited by the War Office to a make a VIP tour of the trenches. He travelled by leave train to the coast and then was conducted aboard one of the boats used for transporting troops. They were all given life jackets (which suddenly made the danger real) and were then accompanied across the Channel by a destroyer. At Boulogne, when he sat down to eat – it had been a very rough crossing and he had not eaten for hours – he was surprised to encounter Captain Higgins of the 1/13th Kensingtons, who invited him to dinner with Colonel Stafford. The next day, after he was given a gas mask to keep with him at all times, he was taken up to Béthune and up the La Bassée Road to trenches east of Cuinchy (little did he know it, but his Fusilier Battalion were in the front line just a couple of miles to the north). It was a lovely day and he was fascinated by the little puff-ball clouds in the sky ('woolly bears' – anti-aircraft fire against German planes). He was given a shock when some British guns right behind him suddenly fired and he was pleasantly surprised to meet a couple of South Kensington men in a dug-out. Next day they took him further north to the trenches around Ploegsteert ('Plugstreet') Wood, where he got a stiff neck from going bent double for several hundred yards along what may have been a front line trench, culminating in a bullet missing him by just a few inches as he stared at the German lines through a trench periscope. He then saw Ploegsteert village heavily shelled by the Germans, shells coming to within about 150 yards of the party. On the next day he was able to meet the men of the 1/13th Kensingtons in a rest camp (rested and reinforced, they were about to join 56th Division) and address them. Already one of the councillors had had a letter back from his son who said that the Mayor's visit had been most inspiring.[74]

When they did get back to official business, they decided to re-appoint most of those who had already worked on local Lord Derby era tribunals, on to the Military Service Tribunals as it was thought their experience would prove useful. Many of the applicants to the tribunals had personal circumstances that made it difficult to join up, such as being sole traders of businesses or having aged parents to look after. For claims such as these the tribunals found it relatively easy to defer conscription for a few months.

On 27th March there was a rather larger crowd than usual at the

Woman Silversmith in
the Peasant Arts shop in
Notting Hill. (ILN)

Kensington Motor-
Driver. (THW)

Drawing of one of the new bus
conductresses that began to be
seen in early 1916. (IWR, AS
Hartrick)

Kensington Van Driver. (THW)

An all-women LCC Ambulance unit. (IWN)

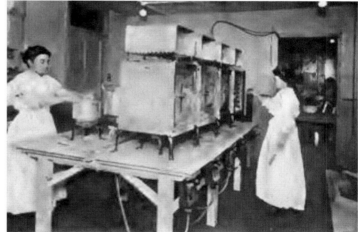

The kitchen of the new T.O.T. Luncheon & Social Club for Women Underground Workers at Earls Court Station. (IWN)

The Recreation Room of the same club. (IWN)

But some were sceptical. The caption went:
Woman Conductor: 'Will you help this man? He won't pay his fare and won't get off the bus.'
Special Constable: 'Er... er... well, how much IS his fare?' (NYTC, after The Bystander)

Kensington Tribunal: word had got out that the cases would be those of conscientious objectors. Members of this particular tribunal were Mayor Davison and Sir Walter Phillimore (both prominent patriots) and Mr Collier (the trade union representative, and more sympathetic to the applicants).

The patriots found it hard to believe that objectors would simply stand by and allow friends and family to be molested if the Germans succeeded in invading. Even if one allowed that this was a valid point of view, how could one distinguish between views genuinely held and those falsely assumed by people who merely did not want to fight?

Six conscientious objectors came from the Central Labour College in Earls Court. Their claim forms had been filled out in an almost identical manner and at least the first three had discussed their testimony in advance, as their answers were so similar. A Mr Williams was the first one interviewed:

Williams, in reply to a question as to what he would do if his mother and sister were being maltreated by the Germans in the case of a successful invasion of this country, which he would do nothing to prevent, said: "I have no reason to suppose that I should do anything to forcibly resist the Germans. I will propose to write to my mother and sister on the subject, and I am quite sure what their reply would be under the circumstances."

Williams said his claim for exemption was based on conscientious and political grounds.

Sir Walter Phillimore pointed out that they could not concern themselves with the political grounds.

The applicant resented the questions that were put to him, but the Mayor observed that as he was asking for a special privilege to be bestowed upon him, it was necessary that the tribunal should investigate very closely the basis on which such a request was made.

He was asked if he had any religious views, and he replied he did not think it necessary to have religious views in order to have a conscience. He had a conscientious objection to taking the life of his fellow men.

Williams said he came from South Wales, and so the Mayor put again the hypothetical case of the Germans landing there and molesting his female relatives. Would his conscience prevent him forcibly interfering with the action of the Germans?

The Applicant: "I should do my duty as a citizen and remain indoors."

The Mayor: "That is not an answer to my questions."

Mr Baxter: "But supposing you were indoors when this molestation of your friends happened, would you stand aside and allow the German troops to do as they liked?"

Applicant: "I think under the circumstances resistance would be useless."[75]

There was no meeting of minds, but the applicants' oblique answers had not helped their case, nor got the audience on their side. Of the six mentioned, four (including Williams) were refused exemption as they had not convinced the panel of the genuineness of their views, but two others were passed for non-combatant service. All said they would appeal. In contrast, the Hammersmith Tribunal had Quaker (Society of Friends) Conscientious Objectors, but an acceptable solution was for them to serve in the Friends Union Ambulance Society (or FAU).[76]

DAVID GREIG.
BACON REDUCED IN PRICE.
Finest Brands Only.
NO HIGHER PRICE.

PRIME BACK, Any Quantity Cut.	1/3
PRIME STREAKY, Any Quantity Cut.	1/2
NUTS AND MILK makes delicious ROMO MARGARINE	7D.
Delicious STANDARD TEA	2/-
Delicious Pure COCOA	4D. Per ½-Pound Tin.

David Greig,
62, HIGH STREET,
Notting Hill.

Despite reduced prices, Back Bacon is 25 per cent up on the 1/- in 1914. (KN)

The Kensington Fusiliers (minus Captain McCausland, who was finding trench life hard at fifty and was sent back to instruct at a Trench Mortar School) had done trench duty in the northern area around Béthune in places such as Givenchy and Festubert, then moved down to the Souchez area (northern part of Vimy Ridge) to take over trenches held by the French. Here both sides' trenches were so vulnerable that the French and the Germans had a private truce. It was said that the Germans opposite were peaceful Saxons who had been sent to this area as a punishment. The Fusiliers tried to slip into the French trenches as quietly as possible, only to hear 'Hello Royal Fusiliers' being shouted at them from a saphead. Sergeant Freddie Pignon remembered:

> *Yes, it was a funny war. We stood behind breastworks – mostly a single row of sandbags which in turn contained chiefly straw and empty tins, and from the shelter of this bulwark we greeted our 'friend the enemy' with a hearty good-morning each day and then he sat on his breastworks and cooked his breakfast and annoyed us, for we dare not even lean against ours without being certain of falling through into the little stretch of 'no man's land' which looked like, and indeed may have been a dumping ground for spare barbed wire.*[77]

They were still in this area, at Hersin, just behind the line, on the 21st May when they saw a free fireworks show coming from the main part of the Vimy Ridge to their right:

In the darkness it was a deluge of flame mingled here and there with such a variety of coloured signals as to outshine any 'Brock's Benefit' that had ever been staged.[78]

Of course it was something much more menacing, a really concentrated German bombardment which succeeded in blasting the 47th Division out of their trenches at the top of the ridge, and captured many of the mine workings that the British had been using literally to undermine the Germans.

99 Brigade were rushed around to the area (part of the way by London buses) to recapture the trenches. The attack was planned for 8.25 pm on the 23rd. The Germans were well aware of the British intentions. Just before they were due to set off, a furious bombardment hit the two attacking battalions of 99 Brigade, the 1st

Vesta Tilley, the most famous male impersonator – excellent in khaki – was on at the Empire in May. Her famous song was 'The army of today's alright'. (Pageant)

Royal Berks and the 22nd Royal Fusiliers. Oddly enough, the two battalions were temporarily being run by their second in commands (Lieutenant Colonel Barker had been acting as temporary Brigade commander). The Berks commander, Major Sharpe, seeing his battalion losing perhaps a hundred men in a few minutes, signalled that he was taking heavy casualties and would not attack. The second-in-command of the 22nd, Major Rostron, signalled back to Brigade that he would conform with the Berks, and not attack either. The units attacking outside 99 Brigade made some lodgements in the German line before being driven out. This was a disaster for 99 Brigade, a huge blunder in their first outing!

This was the impression until someone found out that parts of B

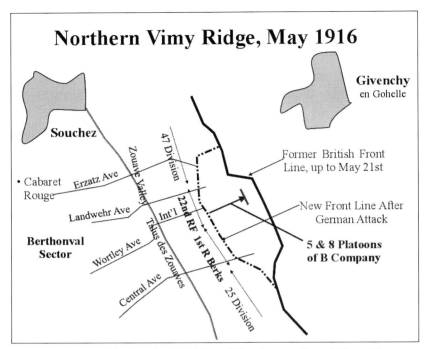

Northern Vimy Ridge, May 1916

Givenchy
en Gohelle

Souchez

47 Division

Zouave Vision

Former British Front
Line, up to May 21st

• Cabaret
Rouge

Erzatz Ave

Landwehr Ave

Int'l

Talus des Zouaves

22nd RF 1st R Berks

New Front Line After
German Attack

Berthonval
Sector

Wortley Ave

Central Ave

25 Division

5 & 8 Platoons
of B Company

Map of the area affecting the 22nd Royal Fusiliers at Vimy Ridge. (A)

Company of the 22nd Fusiliers had not received the recall order, and had set off alone to attack the German trenches, which they then took and held for some considerable time, before the battalion medical officer Captain Miller realised what had happened, scurried across no man's land and found the 22nd attackers consolidating their hold in the German line. He managed, with the greatest difficulty, to persuade the attackers to return to the British lines. Also, after scouring no man's land along with his orderly, he managed to collect every wounded man. He received the DSO for his night's work. Another man decorated afterwards, with the DCM, was Private George Webb from Notting Hill, who remained with his wounded sergeant, although himself wounded in the chest, dressed his wounds under heavy fire, went back to the British lines for stretcher-bearers and refused medical assistance until his sergeant had been attended to.[79]

The Battalion now found that it was being praised for saving the honour of the whole brigade, being the only unit to take German trenches and not be driven out of them. They had won their spurs, at a cost in casualties of three officers and eighty-five other ranks.

The 2/13th Kensingtons thought they were close to going abroad when they arrived in Warminster in January, but they would spend four

NCOs of the 2/13th Kensingtons. (IWN)

months hanging around, feeling forgotten, before being sent west, to Cork, where they arrived to the 'boos and cat-calls of a hostile populace'[80] following the Easter Rebellion. Their task was to help the Royal Irish Constabulary round up known rebels, usually via raids carried out in the dead of night, often in remote and mountainous areas. Back they came in mid-May to be shortly afterwards inspected by first Field Marshal French and then the king – a sign that they really were going abroad. They arrived at Le Havre on 22nd June. A few days later

The Mayor found time to help Kensington win the Inter-Borough Shooting Cup. (B)

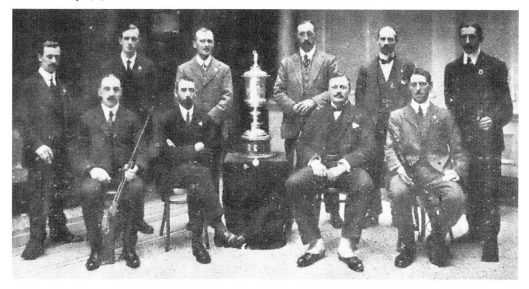

The depot was always short of raw materials, so they had to be creative. (KWHSD, B)

they were based in the ruined village of Neuville St Vaast, behind the Vimy Ridge and a few miles south of where the 22nd Fusiliers had been in action. They would spend the next four months in trench warfare here in what was now a reasonably quiet area of the line, before leaving the Western Front for ever.

By early summer of 1916 the Kensington War Supplies Depot had become a factory. Operating out of six addresses in Kensington Square and one in Cromwell Road, it was producing around 45,000 articles per week and supplying 300 hospitals in Britain and abroad. Some 5,000 women workers were on their books, of whom around 1,200 worked every day. They could, it was said, turn just about anything into just about anything.

May 21st at 2 am was the hour when the first ever British Summer Time began. Mr Willett had been arguing since 1907 that it would harmonise the hours of daylight with those of work better; but the key argument now was that it would save precious fuel. As 'the' weekend

Less expected at the Depot were the women welders. (WI, WP, B)

And women blacksmiths. (ILN, WI, B)

They were successful at getting publicity in many newspapers and magazines, but were still obliged to put on fund-raising events. (KWHSD, B)

Mr Willett of daylight saving time fame. (Pageant)

Time itself was being changed (and the Germans had beaten us to it by a fortnight). (THW)

approached, people were worried by aspects such as if you were booked to work the night shift from midnight to 8 am, should you work the clock times – or do the eight hours expected of you? Then the local paper reminded everyone that the Borough of Kensington, earlier convinced by the arguments of Mr Willett's scheme, had quietly been operating Daylight Saving hours in their municipal offices for the last two years.

The event passed off quietly. Far more emotive and persistent was the enemy aliens question. On 26th June there was a long procession, with musical accompaniment, from Hammersmith Broadway to Kensington Town Hall where a 'well-filled hall' awaited the British Empire Union making a powerful resolution concerning:

> *... the rigorous exclusion of all enemy aliens from prohibited areas and from Government employment. And also that all subjects of the Central European Powers resident in this country should be interned whether previously interned or not.*

The principal speaker was Ernest Wild KC. Among his cheer-generating remarks was:

> *Crushing the Prussian beast so effectually in the interests of humanity that he may never raise his head again. He went further: In his opinion, and the opinion of the British Empire Union, the most dangerous German in this country was the naturalised one.*[81]

Not the most forgiving or tolerant organisation. (WC, David Wilson, 1918)

Of course the resolution was passed unanimously.

At around the same time the Kensington Chamber of Commerce was also meeting in the Town Hall and debating a very similar resolution, also passed. Inevitably, similar resolutions came up at the next Kensington Borough Council meeting. The Mayor tried to derail one of the motions, and Sir Walter Phillimore attempted to put the common-sense view that some naturalised Germans had done great credit to this country, but the hot-headed position that 'it was impossible to make a German a gentleman by naturalisation' prevailed. Fortunately the recommendations were then simply passed along the line to the Government, allowing the steam to hiss away.

In contrast, on 11th July Lord Derby unveiled a memorial at Brompton Cemetery for Sub-Lieutenant RAJ Warneford, who had so excited the nation by destroying a Zeppelin near Ostend in June 1915 but then died in a flying accident a few days later.

On 1st July the Battle of the Somme began in France. Both the 2/13th Kensingtons and the 22nd Fusiliers were fortunate to miss the first phase of the battle. The 1/13th Kensingtons, on the other hand, were part of the diversionary attack at Gommecourt, a mile or so beyond the left (north) flank of the battle. At Gommecourt, the German

Lord Derby about to unveil the memorial at Brompton Cemetery. (IWN)

COURAGE
INITIATIVE INTREPIDITY
FLIGHT-SUB-LIEUT-REGINALD
ALEXANDER-JOHN-WARNEFORD
V.C·R.N.A.S.·BORN·15·OCT·1891
ACCIDENTALLY·KILLED·17·JUNE·1915

The Warneford memorial in 2013. The letters have been re-cut (but not those at the bottom of the memorial that say that the money was raised by Daily Express readers). (A)

front line stuck out in a great bulge or salient. The 56th (London) Division (containing 1/13th Kensingtons) were to attack from the south-west and the 46th (North Midland) Division from the north-west. Ideally, they would meet behind Gommecourt village, having lanced the boil. The Kensingtons were to support the London Scottish at the extreme right-hand flank, and their job would be to follow up the Scottish and protect them and their gains.

Although the 56th Division attack went well initially, with almost all units reaching their first objectives and some men reaching past their second objectives almost to the junction point, that for the 46th Division did not. It encountered uncut wire and an alert enemy; almost all of the attacks were beaten back before they got to the German lines.

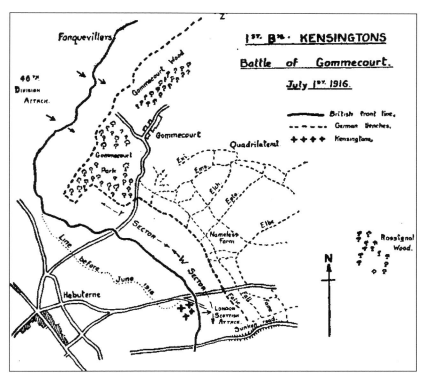

Map to show the Battle of Gommecourt. (TK)

That meant that the Germans were able to concentrate their resources on driving the 56th Division out of their trenches. By late afternoon the remnants of their attacks were also back in the British lines. The Kensingtons lost nearly half their (reduced) fighting strength in casualties: sixteen officers and 300 men.

By 27th July it was the turn of the Kensington Fusiliers. Despite its fairly disastrous first day, the Battle of the Somme had raged on. Some considerable success was won in a daring night attack on 14th July, which enabled the South African Brigade of 9th Division to take Delville Wood – ground the Germans were very reluctant to yield. After several days of desperate defence, the South Africans had been driven right back to the extreme south-east of it. It became 99 Brigade's job to recapture it. A very powerful bombardment enabled the 1st KRRC and the 23rd Royal Fusiliers, followed by the 1st Royal Berks in support, to storm and occupy the wood very quickly and efficiently. But their troubles were just beginning. The Germans set up attack after attack. Anywhere they were not attacking was subjected to a non-stop bombardment. The 22nd Royal Fusiliers, having had a main role in the last attack, were the reserve battalion. Nevertheless, every available man of the 22nd – and any other unit close enough, including engineers and sappers – was dragged into the fighting. Those 22nd men that could be found were relieved on the night of the 27th/28th; a few, tucked away in the remains of the wood, itself reduced to stumps and a mass of shell holes, could not be reached for some days.

A few days later the Battalion got the job that no one wanted, that of garrisoning the wood, still under continuous artillery fire. This time, by bravely doing two personal reconnaissances across the whole wood, and reorganising its defence via the use of heavy and light machine guns rather than vulnerable human beings, Colonel Barker (who would receive the DSO for his work) was able to ensure that the Battalion's time in the wood incurred only a handful of casualties. Overall they had lost eight officers and 259 other ranks, including Captain Allan MacDougall – killed in the final relief, just as he had scrawled down 'Relief Complete'.

Private 'Dad' Grover, that over-age man who had arrived in a chauffeured Rolls Royce every day in the White City days, also lost his life here, blown up by a shell when staying on in the wood to care for a wounded man.

Colonel Barker had previously attempted to write to the family of every man killed, but the sheer numbers of casualties made that unworkable here. Instead, a list was sent to the Mayor, who then attempted to send a more humane letter to the next of kin, and which was quicker than the official communication. As he wrote to the Colonel:

> *I am glad you sent me the list of casualties. I wrote to the next of kin of all the men killed whose addresses I had, and have received very grateful letters from them. Most of them do not appear to have previously received any intimation of their relatives' deaths in action, so it is as well I wrote.*[82]

On 21st-23rd August the film *The Battle of the Somme* was shown in

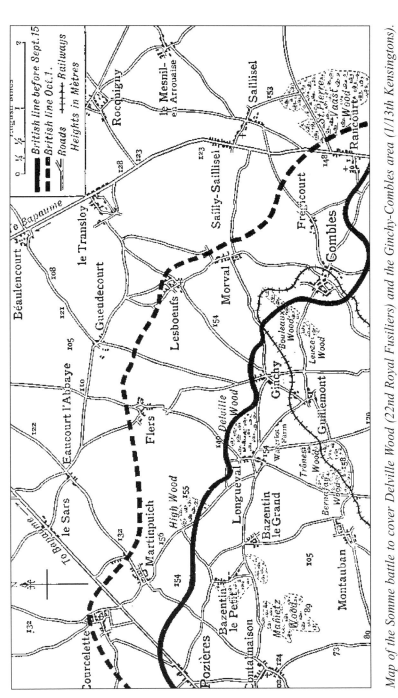

Map of the Somme battle to cover Delville Wood (22nd Royal Fusiliers) and the Ginchy-Combles area (1/13th Kensingtons). (TGWW)

the Silver Cinema in the Uxbridge Road and astounded Kensington audiences (as elsewhere in Britain) who had little idea what 'The Front' was really like. The *Kensington News* went just a little too far:

> *It is indisputable that never since its advent has the Cinema contributed a more notable service to the world at large than in the presentation of the Official War Picture depicting the Great Somme Battle, in addition to striking episodes and incidents taking place at the Front.*[83]

The Military Tribunals continued. Some were easy, like the actor who simply asked for a month's exemption to train his understudy. Men came in from their place of work still smelling of whatever they were doing. This was most pleasant in the case of the wood-working machinist, still exuding a fragrant smell of pinewood, but there were others:

> *Soon the odour of another kind smote their nostrils. A fish curer walked in, and the need for pocket handkerchiefs was at once noticeable.*[84]

The 1/13th Kensingtons were in action again in September and October in the area of Ginchy and Combles, only a mile or two to the right of Delville Wood. On 9th September they were sucked into an unsuccessful attack to the east of Ginchy to eliminate a German strong point called the Quadrilateral. This proved to be too strongly defended; amongst the casualties was Major CC Dickens (grandson of Charles Dickens). They were in reserve for the attack that finally cleared Combles on 24th September. Finally, their Brigade made little progress in featureless conditions and atrocious weather east of Lesboeufs on 7th October. At last, only a fraction of their former numbers, they moved away from the Somme and back to the Estaires area where they first went into the trenches in 1914.

By October, presumably influenced by recent heavy losses in France, the mood in the tribunal court had changed; the need for men now trumped everything, so it was now very difficult for men aged under thirty to get exemption for any reason, whether they were married or single. Indeed the military representatives now suggested

Mayor Davison, looking comfortable in his VTC uniform, in a party to assess the defences of London. (B)

The Punch caption reads:
Mistress (coming to maid's room as the Zeppelins approach): 'Jane! Jane! Won't you come downstairs with the rest of us?
Little Maid: 'Oh, thankyou, but I can see beautiful from here, Mum.' (Blighty, after Punch)

re-examining earlier exemptions (and any class B or C medical classifications, enabling men to escape the Front) to see if the reasons were still valid. Towards the end of the year there would be a number of prosecutions for doctors and recruiters giving class C certificates for money.

On 2nd September came the event that all who had lived under the shadow of the Zeppelin must have yearned for. The editor of the *Kensington News* was admirably placed, being out of doors in the early hours of the morning in North London at the Broadway (presumably the Broadway in Crouch Hill):

> *A night of dense, heavy vapours.*
>
> *Trams crawling like sleepy glow-worms, their lights shrouded to mere pin points. Over the street hangs a double pall, the blackness overhead, the silence of midnight, broken only by here and there the voice of some stray belated reveller...*
>
> *Boom! Hark! It's coming! Nothing to see, nothing to hear, save now and then boom! and the mutter of the groups assembling in the street and spaces like the Broadway.*
>
> *"They're coming. They're being fired at." Now and again a duller, thudding sound. The midnight stragglers increase in number and in animation. More Specials hurry stationwards. Nearer comes the sound of firing. Once or twice in the dense black of the sky there is the glint as of minute splinters of silver glass...*
>
> *Boom! Oh, if a shot could only reach the marauder of the air. Ah, if only! Dash it! – The angry mutter goes on in a muted monotone.*
>
> *Look! Look there! Fire! Fire!*
>
> *What have they fired? Something! One answers with an icy thrill one's own question, for of a sudden there is a quivering glow in the sky yonder. The northern Broadway buildings stand silhouetted clear black against it: people, police, specials are scampering forward. Other shouts go up: "There she is! Look, look!"*
>
> *Joining the rush, we share in the sight – we join in the handclapping, the shouting, the frenzied "Hurrah! Hurrah! Hurrah!"*

Some thought the airship 'like a new incandescent gas mantle when first lighted'. (CHW after The Sphere)

For now we are in full sight of a spectacle for tragedy, grandeur and wonder surpassing all we have seen on or off any stage, read of in any book of romance or reality, fancied in the most fantastic dream.

Then mid-high in the now lurid glowing heavens we behold the Zeppelin, posed at a downward angle, her lower half glowing like a huge blunt-ended cube of iron red hot in a furnace, the upper wreathed in an ever increasing and widening sheaf of lurid flames. Spontaneously we realise that she has met her fate. The Destroyer is being destroyed, helplessly, surely, before our eyes. Those who came out to demolish by fire are by fire being demolished.

Awhile she glides and sways helplessly, hopeless along, glowing and flaming more quickly. Then she makes a forward cant and plunges downwards in a nose air dive. We wait for the sound of an anticipated detonating roar that does not come, and we know that the Zeppelin is dead.[85]

Using the newly developed incendiary bullets, Lieutenant William Leefe Robinson was the first man to shoot down an airship over Britain. He, too, was awarded the VC, plus around £3,500 reward money. Relics of the airship, made into brooches, bangles, rings and so on, ensured a very successful flag day for the Red Cross in October, the relics raising over £100 at the stall in central Kensington.

Lieutenant Leefe Robinson, the first man to bring down a 'Zeppelin' (actually a Schütte-Lanz) over Britain. (IWN)

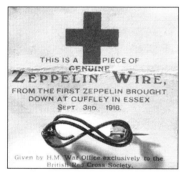

That which was not made into brooches etc, was cut into even smaller pieces to raise money for the Red Cross, while an exhibition of Zeppelin relics was held at Finsbury. (B)

There was lots of metal debris... (THW)

The ruins of L33 – lightly burned compared to the others. The Mayor acquired his own copy of this striking picture. (B)

Londoners would not have to wait long for a second success against the Zeppelins: L33 was forced down and its crew apprehended by a Special Constable in the early hours of 24th September, while another one was shot down near Potters Bar on the evening of 1st October. Michael MacDonagh, reporting for *The Times*, and therefore armed with the additional information that this was L31, commanded by the redoubtable Commander Mathy, was sent up to Potters Bar to see the body. He did not feel at all exultant when he saw it, and the huge indentation it had made in the ground as a result of him choosing to jump from the burning airship rather than await being burnt to death. Instead he commented:

> *Be it remembered also that he, like hundreds of thousands of other young men, in all the belligerent countries, was caught in the toils of the War that was not of his making or theirs.*[86]

Thousands of curious onlookers packed all the trains up from London on 2nd October to see the debris (little knowing that the police and military had now cordoned the area off).

Commanders Mathy (L31) and Petersen (L32) jumped out of their airships rather than wait for the flames to engulf them. (WI)

The Notting Hill Coronet had closed as a theatre but reopened as a cinema: a growing trend. In contrast, the Shepherd's Bush Empire's cartoon Bushman Family advertisements had now become so popular that the family featured in their own show. Readers of the *Kensington News* who had turned to page 6 to read the weekly Bushman Family cartoon, were told:

Important Announcement
The Bushman Family (Mr, Mrs, Dolly and Reggie) have kindly accepted the invitation of the Manager of the Shepherd's Bush Empire to appear in a big revue on Monday October 16th and twice nightly during the week.[87] *Life imitating art!*

The Bushman Family come to life. Of course the patriotic Mr Bushman has an exemption, is a Special Policeman and a Volunteer (member of VTC), and now he can add that he is doing special work for the Empire. (KN)

In the week following their appearance, Mr Bushman was given most of the advertising space on page 6 to thank those who had come to see them:

Mr and Mrs Bushman beg to thank the thousands of visitors to the Bush Theatre last week, for the kindly interest they took in the Family's first appearance on the stage.[88]

Mr. and Mrs. Bushman and family beg to thank the thousands of visitors to the Bush Empire last week, for the kindly interest they took in the Family's first appearance on the stage. They also wish to take this opportunity of thanking the Management for the opportunity of appearing on one of the finest stages in London—an opportunity they would not have missed for worlds. Their love for the Bush Entertainment is emphasised in no small degree by the kindness shown to them.

(Signed) Mr. BUSHMAN.

The Bushman Family thank their patrons. (KN)

There was one final act of the Somme battle to be completed in the area of the Ancre Valley. It had been practised and then cancelled repeatedly throughout most of October because of extremely wet weather. There were just enough dry days in early November and the attack began on the 13th. 2nd Division were roughly in the middle of this attack. The formation north of them, 3rd Division, failed, and this affected 6 Brigade. The unit south of them, 51st (Highland) Division, stormed Beaumont Hamel and 5 Brigade made some good progress next to them. The 22nd Royal Fusiliers' job was to create a defensive flank to protect the gains made

More and more days were flag days for something. This is 'Our Day' for the wounded. (B)

by 5 Brigade. That done, the Battalion was asked to take on the big German strong point called the Quadrilateral (not the one faced by 1/13th Kensingtons; but just as feared). On 15th November, men of the 22nd Royal Fusiliers under Major Phythian-Adams, (reinforced by parties from a number of different battalions) occupied and controlled enough of it to make the Germans flee. Overall the Battalion lost five officers and eighty-two other ranks, including Sergeant HH Munro, better known as Saki, the short story writer. After their efforts they were sent back to Yvrench, near Abbeville, where they would spend a memorable Christmas well away from the fighting.

Sergeant H.H. Munro, alias the short-story writer, Saki.

The 2/13th Kensingtons, as part of 60th Division, believed they were about to be sent to the Somme but found themselves on a seemingly endless (55-hour) train journey to Marseille, where they embarked on HMT *Transylvania* for a relaxing voyage to Salonika, reached on 30th November. It was not a popular place: 'It proved to be the filthiest and most uninteresting place so far encountered on their travels.'[89] Ten days later they were taken aboard the cruiser HMS *Endymion* and made an amphibious landing near the town of Katerina, which guarded Salonika from the south. This was in case Greece changed its mind about which side it was fighting on. Prime Minister Venizelos was pro-Entente, while King Constantine was pro-German. After a few months this danger was considered over and the 60th Division marched forward to the trenches at the Doiran Front, where they would stay until mid-summer 1917.

The Kensington population had become accustomed to seeing female bus and tram conductors, even to spotting the occasional female policeman, but in Notting Hill Gate a new training school was opened to train women as oxy-acetylene welders. It took about five or six weeks for the training, and the students could then move on to lucrative jobs on aircraft manufacturing.

In November Mayors Davison and Foreman were again returned unopposed in Kensington and Hammersmith, as was Mayor Norris in

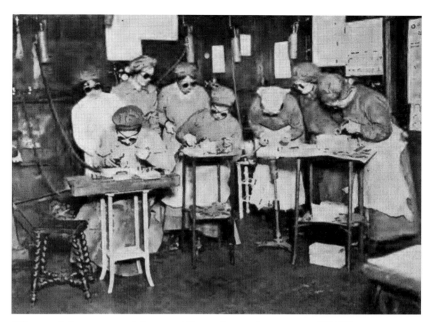

Women doing oxy-acetylene welding of aeroplane parts. (THW)

Fulham. With good men in power and party politics set aside, why change them?

Road Safety results for Kensington in 1914–1916 were published in November and demonstrated a huge increase in deaths from 1914 to 1915, for which the most obvious reason was the lack of street lighting. The dark streets continued in 1916 and these figures were close to 1915 levels, with perhaps a small decrease as people got accustomed to taking more care or of venturing out less after dark.

Killed by:	Tramcar	Motor Omnibus	Other (Cars etc)	Total
1914	37	148	308	493
1915	86	154	426	666
1916				
Jan-Oct	63	135	311	509
	(76^)	(162^)	(373^)	(^611)

^Annual equivalent, ie the results for the 10 months multiplied by 12/10, which will be an under-estimate because November and December are both dark months.

Walking on the pavements at night could be a very dangerous thing, especially if one came across a dog-walker who had kept to the (outer) right hand side of the pavement, as officially requested, but had allowed the dog to investigate the infinitely more attractive scents on the left (inside) of the pavement, thus creating an ambulating tripwire. In fact dogs were receiving some glowering looks; did they justify their retention in these days of food shortages? As the *Kensington News* put it delicately:

> *There are said to be canine pessimists who apprehend meatless days not only arriving, but being followed by dog days.*

One particular dog got its owner into potentially very hot water. Sir Edward Henry had been the Commissioner of the Metropolitan Police since 1903. He made a number of innovations in policing, including the introduction of fingerprinting, detective and uniformed training schools and police dogs. He was close to retirement when the war broke out but had stayed on out of duty. He used to walk the long distance between his home in Kensington and Scotland Yard, probably accompanied by his Scottie. Due to a combination of his wound (a disgruntled failed taxi driver had attempted to assassinate him in 1912) and his age (upper sixties) he switched over to using the Underground. One day he was stopped on the steps down to his local station by one of the new female Inspectors, who asked him if he had a ticket for his dog:

Caricature of Sir Edward Henry and dog, but not the Scottie in the story. (by Spy, in Vanity Fair 1905)

> *"No," Sir Edward said. "He's only quite a little chap and I didn't think a ticket was needed for him. In fact, I didn't even know that he was there. He must have followed me from home without my knowing it."*
>
> *"I'm afraid I shall have to report this," the lady said. "Could I have your name and address, please?"*

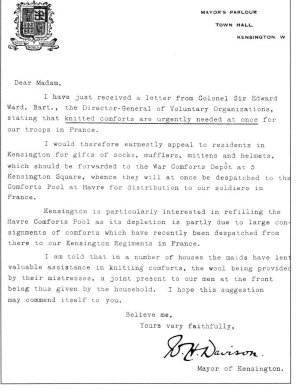

MAYOR'S PARLOUR
TOWN HALL,
KENSINGTON. W

Dear Madam,

I have just received a letter from Colonel Sir Edward Ward, Bart., the Director-General of Voluntary Organizations, stating that <u>knitted comforts are urgently needed at once</u> for our troops in France.

I would therefore earnestly appeal to residents in Kensington for gifts of socks, mufflers, mittens and helmets, which should be forwarded to the War Comforts Depôt at 5 Kensington Square, whence they will at once be despatched to the Comforts Pool at Havre for distribution to our soldiers in France.

Kensington is particularly interested in refilling the Havre Comforts Pool as its depletion is partly due to large consignments of comforts which have recently been despatched from there to our Kensington Regiments in France.

I am told that in a number of houses the maids have lent valuable assistance in knitting comforts, the wool being provided by their mistresses, a joint present to our men at the front being thus given by the household. I hope this suggestion may commend itself to you.

Believe me,
Yours very faithfully,

Mayor of Kensington.

The sort of begging letter one would only see in a rich borough like Kensington: rich owner buys the wool, and the servants do the knitting: everyone contributes, but one hopes the servants were not expected to do the knitting in their own time! (B)

Headlines like 'Police Chief a Fare Cheat' could have resulted, but someone cleverly found a way out, and sent Sir Edward a special season ticket for the whole of the Underground, for the duration of the life of the person it was issued to, that person being 'Sir Edward Henry's dog.' The dog ended up as a celebrity in its own right. It used to sit by the feet of the policeman directing the streams of traffic at Whitehall (close to Scotland Yard), calmly watching until it worked out how the system worked. As soon as the correct stream had been held up, it would trot happily across the road. Of course the constables on duty were desperately keen that nothing happened to the chief's dog on their watch – sometimes to the detriment of the flow of the normal traffic. [90]

Now that three Kensington battalions were abroad on active service, the number of cigarettes sent by the Mayor/Mayoress/ Kensington Council as Christmas presents had gone up to 170,000.[91]

1916 ended. There had been enormous casualties among the new Kitchener Army volunteers and Territorials alike, and a big naval battle against the German fleet (Jutland), but the end seemed no nearer. Perhaps many men felt like Lewis gunner Paul Destrubé:

> *Twelve months have I passed here, and my nerves are not what they were, but still now I feel fortified to stand the strain of another long year of this campaign.*[92]

At home the Zeppelin menace was less scary now that a few of them had been shot down. There was darkness and drabness instead of colour, but the incomparable Marie Lloyd was on at the Bush Empire for Christmas week, so one could lose oneself in merriment for a few hours. And there were occasional moments that just made one feel good to be alive. Thus at the 'ordinarily drab atmosphere' of the West London Police Court, an elderly man was had up on 15th December for the crime of begging in a public place. He had attempted to attract attention by taking with him a cage containing a blackbird and a thrush – and the cage with its occupants had been borne along to court with due dignity:

> *And the kindly cadi* [the Worshipful Mr Francis], *noting they were beating their wings against the bars, decreed their release, and in reply to the accused's contention that they had only been "catched" a week, declared that this was a week too long.*

Constable 382T was deputed to take the cage to Holland Park and release the birds and, as a final act of Christmas mercy, the magistrate released the beggar also.[93]

CHAPTER 4

1917

The Premier has stated that the submarine menace
is being dealt with

December's health statistics showed a very large increase in deaths in the Borough, many of which were bronchial and pneumonic in character, and so it was thought that the heavy fogs over the Christmas period had 'carried off' many older residents.

In early February the Germans began unrestricted submarine warfare, with the immediate result that Britain needed to import less and grow more of its own food. Some twenty acres of land in Kensington were made available by the Borough for private cultivation in small plots. In fact the local paper soon began a column of advice for new allotment holders (and the whole Bushman Family was pictured having fun digging and planting vegetables in their newly acquired allotment).

The Mayor urged everyone to buy the new 'Victory' War Loan; whereas earlier Loans seemed more for larger investors, just sixpence was enough to start a War Savings Certificate, and he said that your money would go straight to buying munitions for our brave boys at the Front. The idea was to get the largest possible number of people to invest. Big employers like Harrods offered to buy £5 or £10 of War Bonds for their employees, who could then pay the company back at two or four shillings a week. Even on the penultimate day of the campaign, the Mayor was sharing a platform with Will Thorne MP in Trafalgar Square and passionately declaiming, as only he could, that this loan had to be 'the greatest financial success of any effort of its

War Loan Rally in Trafalgar Square. (ILN, B)

kind in the world' in order to show the Germans just how determined the British people were to see this thing through.

While the cartoon Mr Bushman was pictured addressing a War Loan meeting, the *real* Mr Bushman, alias Sir William Bull MP, one of Hammersmith's most famous figures, interrupted a performance at the Bush Empire (along with Betty Barclay, one of that week's stars) to make a 'forcible appeal' to the audience – and raised £681 from them.

War Loan continued. Primus inter pares! The other Mayors (including the Lord Mayor) look like small, slumping men with straggling moustaches, whereas Mayor Davison stands up ramrod straight. (B)

Sir William Bull and his 'Bushmen', more properly called the 20th (Hammersmith Battalion) County of London Volunteer Regiment. (WC)

The Loan was a very attractive investment at its 5 per cent interest rate and an enormous amount (over £2 billion) was raised by it, although just over half of this was from canny investors transferring from earlier Loans at 3½ per cent to 4½ per cent. Kensington Borough seemingly scraped up every spare penny to invest £92,000 in it.[94]

The London General Omnibus Company had begun a campaign of paternalistic pieces of advice in rhyme, but the company's drivers were themselves not without sin, as the *Kensington News* commented:

The LGOC: full of practical suggestions for the public. (KN)

> *Jack and Jill toiled up the hill,*
> *Their journey had been shorter;*
> *But the bus past flew*
> *Though with room for two,*
> *And Jill sighed, "He didn't oughter."*[95]

On 16th February, Paul Destrubé of the Kensington Fusiliers was writing to his Marion, and drew a vivid picture:

> *Tonight we have managed to find with difficulty some wood with which we have kindled a cheery fire. Oh smoky fire, how pleasant it is to share thy warmth! Close up to these I crouch and in the flickering light I pen these lines to the very dearest of my friends. The morrow brings strife, but tonight must speak of peace, because my thoughts, as they so often are, are with you. The flames are darting hither and thither – the joyful companion of my thoughts – and as I watch them gaily dancing my thoughts drift back to England and to you.*
>
> *There are four of us round this fire and, with the exception of myself, they are holding their fingers bent with cold over the flames. One of their number had been too free with the rum bottle. And consequently is rather talkative. He is relating his experiences of his civilian employment as a dustman. At times I*

lay aside my pen to warm up and catch glimpses of his comical and humorous anecdotes. He is telling us about some tender confidences, with an illustration of the accompanying hugs etc, he once made to a servant girl, and the sensational entrance of the mistress of the house. Then he draws the rum bottle from his pocket, and it goes round from mouth to mouth…

Good-bye cheery fire, thanks for your warmth! The dustman chap is asleep, his head rests on his chest and every now and then he nearly overbalances into the brazier. The others have rolled themselves up in their blankets and sleep deep upon the ground. I'll follow them. Good-night, dear Marion, may your bed be softer than mine.[96]

This would be Paul's last letter.

One result of the terrible fighting that had gone on for four months in the Battle of the Somme was that the Germans did not want to be involved in a repeat of that battle. Over the winter they had been building a new, very strong, trench system some 25 miles further back, and their plan was to move into it in March. Once the Allies got wind of it, they were determined to scotch the German plans. Consequently an attack was planned for 17th February in the Miraumont area for 18th and 2nd Divisions to drive the Germans out of their trenches. 99 Brigade was in the centre, with the KRRC attacking initially on the left and 23rd Royal Fusiliers on the right. The 22nd were to help the KRRC and take over from them in the move from second to third objectives, and to create a defensive flank on the right hand side of the attack to protect the advances of the 23rd Royal Fusiliers. At the last moment a great thaw happened, making the firm ground greasy, while one or more deserters from a neighbouring unit went over to the Germans, giving them a considerable amount of detail about the attack. So, just before the commencement of the battle, a huge bombardment came down on the men crowded in and just in front of the British lines. The British did manage to get forward to their first objectives, and some reached their second objectives, but counter-attacks by the newly reinforced Germans drove them back. At one stage it all depended on a small party of D Company of the 22nd, led by Lance-Sergeant Fred Palmer. If they were driven in, then all the British gains would have been lost. Palmer and his men resisted eight German attacks over three hours. As a result, he was commissioned in the field and recommended for the Victoria Cross.

The 22nd Fusiliers were in the thick of many parts of the battle, and this would be by far their largest total of casualties. We do not know the exact number – it's around 270–275 men and twelve officers – because the efficient casualty information system created by Mayor Davison and Lieutenant Colonel Barker had been stamped on by the War Office.

Paul Destrubé and his brother Guy were Lewis gunners, particular targets of the Germans. Almost three in four of them became casualties in this battle. Paul and Guy died in each other's arms and were buried in the same grave in Serre Road Number 1 Cemetery, with the moving inscription: *'Unis dans la mort comme ils l'étaient dans la vie.'*[97]

The three Destrubé brothers, Georges, Paul and Guy. George got a 'Blighty One' in 1916. (B, 8369)

One long-debated topic moved towards a resolution, as the Speaker's Conference on Electoral Reform voted in favour of 'some measure of woman suffrage'. It did not feel dramatic enough, but as a result of this decision (some) women (over thirty) would be able to vote in the next election.

The new Food Controller, Lord Davenport, suggested a voluntary limit on the amount of meat consumed, at 5½ ounces of meat per person per day. One way around this would be to have a meatless day now and again in order to save up one's meat allowance to have a

Poor potato harvests here and abroad in 1916 led to shortages and long queues everywhere. (this in North London, THW)

The first Food Controller Lord Davenport. (Peel, Cup)

Demonstration of potato spraying in Kensington Gardens under the watchful eyes of the Ministry of Agriculture. (IWN)

reasonably large portion. Another way, suggested by Short & Sons of Notting Hill and CE Betts & Son of Kensington High Street in the front page of the local paper, was that if you are going to eat only small quantities of meat, then let it be of the finest quality, which of course was what they supplied. Unfortunately, it did seem that some food retailers took advantage of the scheme to charge enhanced prices for staple items. As the *Kensington News* put it:

> *Appeals to their conscience are in vain, for their avarice has killed such conscience as they ever knew.*[98]

Lord Davenport was obliged to bring in maximum prices for a variety of items such as tea, butter and lard. He employed two Directors of Women's Service, Mrs CS (Dorothy) Peel and Mrs (Maud) Pember Reeves (author of the famous social study *Round About a Pound a Week*). They had to create their own jobs: their duties would include designing war cookery recipes in the new kitchen at Grosvenor House and getting millions of Food Economy leaflets printed and distributed; there was 'feeding the press' and replying to thousands of letters, but by far the dominant duty was addressing meetings. Dorothy Peel counted up 176 meetings that she addressed in the twelve months from March 1917.[99] Several of these were in Kensington, where she took rather a shine to the Mayor ('a very fine figure of a man').

The first of these was The British Women's Patriotic League's well-attended meeting at the Town Hall on *Food Rations and Housekeeping* on

Honour Bound!

'expresses what we feel with regard to carrying out Lord Devonport's food limitations. Since we may only eat a small quantity of meat it is of the utmost importance that the meat we do buy should be of the very first quality. For best quality means maximum nourishment.

In spite of present difficulties our long buying experience enables us to maintain our reputation for supplying the very finest meat. Moreover, our Poultry and Fish Department will help you to fill in your menu so that it shall not exceed the Devonport Meat Allowance. Finally, our Weekly Special Offer will help you to keep down expenditure.

Don't you feel you ought to deal with us? Our 'phone number is 1935 Park and our name and address '

**SHORT & SONS, Ltd.,
15, 17, 19, High St.,
Notting Hill Gate.**

Short & Sons could claim to be the leading specialist butcher, and they were certainly the most outspoken. (KN)

Mrs C.S. Peel (Dorothy); wonderfully talented on all aspects of domestic economy. (Peel, Cup)

March 2nd (arranged before her Directorial appointment). After a glowing introduction by the Mayor, Dorothy Peel gave a stirring speech:

> *Hitherto length of purse, taste and appetite decided what we should eat and how we should live. That was at an end now. We had only two things to think of – to eat that we might live and to conserve our strength for the work we had to do for England. That being so, it became necessary to learn how much we must eat and how much we must not eat. There were many anxious people who feared that if we keep to the ration system we should become underfed...*
>
> *The general public must be made to understand that it was not merely a question of eating a little less meat, bread and sugar, and a great deal more of other foods, but only of consuming just sufficient of whatever food was chosen to keep themselves in health for the work they had to perform.*

The Royal Borough of Kensington War Savings Committee

HAVE ARRANGED A

PUBLIC MEETING

IN THE

KENSINGTON TOWN HALL

On Friday, March 30th, at 3 p.m.

IN THE CHAIR

THE MAYOR OF KENSINGTON

SPEAKERS

Mrs. C. S. PEEL

AND

Mrs. PEMBER REEVES

The Directors of Women's Service, Ministry of Food

"Patriotic Housekeeping"

AND

"The Reasons for Voluntary Rations"

ADMISSION FREE   QUESTIONS

Arrangements will be made for an overflow meeting in the Small Hall, if necessary

Mrs Peel returns by popular demand, this time with Mrs Pember Reeves. (B)

She concluded:

> *We at home were asking of the men at the front endurance and sacrifice almost beyond understanding...and now we were asked to make a further effort to work harder, spend less, to live more sparingly and, if it should be necessary, even to undergo real privation. And surely the women of England could face that with courage, determination, and endurance for the love of God, of this dear England, and of all those men who had already made such great sacrifices to the cause. (Applause)*[100]

From the audience (perhaps someone cognizant of the growing losses being suffered by our Merchant Navy due to U-boats) came a suggestion for a new Grace: *For what we are allowed to receive may we be loyally thankful to God, our country, and our brave sailors.*

We risk our lives to bring you food. It's up to you not to waste it.

"A Message from our Seamen"

A word from the seamen about not wasting food. (IWR)

STANDARD PARCELS OF FOOD.
GERMANY.

As a result of the past three months' experience, the Central Prisoners of War Committee has decided to revise the contents of the Standard Parcels to be sent to Prisoners of War in Germany. As before, three of these parcels will ordinarily be sent per fortnight to each man. The serious rise in the cost of provisions has compelled us to raise the price of these parcels from 6s. to 7s., but we do not propose at present to charge 7s. to those "Adopters" who are already on our books or to Care Committees for whom we are packing. We recommend other Care Committees to adopt a similar standard, and we would bring to their notice the urgent necessity of providing parcels which contain at any rate the equivalent food value whatever the price may be.

A

1 lb. Beef
½ lb. Vegetables (Cabbage, Brussels Sprouts, Turnips or Carrots)
1 Tin Rations
¼ lb. Cheese (Tin)
¼ lb. Tea
½ lb. Nestlé's Milk
¾ lb. Sugar
¼ lb. Margarine
1 lb. Jam
1 lb. Biscuits
50 Cigarettes
1 Tin Sardines

B

1 Tin Sausages
1 Tin Herrings
1 Tin Oxo Cubes or Marmite
1 lb. Biscuits
¼ lb. Tin Cocoa
¾ lb. Cooked Ham
¼ lb. Dripping
1 Tin Baked Beans
50 Cigarettes
¾ lb. Nestlé's Milk
1 Tin Syrup
Pepper, Salt, Mustard
Knight's Carbolic Soap

C

1 Tin Beef
1 Tin Salmon
½ lb. Ration Biscuits
¼ lb. Tin Milk
¼ lb. Tea
¼ lb. Sugar
1 Tin Fruit
1 Tin Oxo Cubes
¼ lb. Grape Nuts or Force
¾ lb. Figs, Chocolate or Dates
1 Tin Potted Meat
Small Suet Pudding
½ lb. Margarine or Dripping
1 Tablet Soap

D

1 Tin Beef or Rations
½ lb. Ham (in tin)
1 Tin Sardines
1 Tin Baked Beans
3 Soup Squares
¼ lb. Tea
¼ lb. Sugar
¼ lb. Tin Nestlé's Milk
¼ lb. Brawn Paté or Camp Pie
¼ lb. Biscuits
¼ lb. Dripping
¼ lb. Currant Biscuits
50 Cigarettes
1 lb. Tin Marmalade

Examples of Red Cross parcels being sent in 1917. (B)

Mrs Peel (this time accompanied by Mrs Pember Reeves) was invited back on 30th March, with Carillon commenting:

Both of the Directors of Women's Service are fluent speakers, and it was a pleasure as well as an education to listen to them.

In early April Mayor Davison discovered another responsibility connected with raising a battalion: acting as liaison between Prisoners of War, their families and the requisite authorities, such as the Central Prisoners of War Committee (based in Thurloe Place, South Kensington) of the British Red Cross Society, in order to get them supplied with regular food parcels (and, later, other perishables and clothing).

In the confused to-and-fro fighting on February 17th, twenty-four men, including one officer, were taken prisoner, most of them wounded.[101] It was a great comfort to both prisoners and their families to know that their Mayor had their interests at heart and, even better, knew exactly what to do to get comforts to their relatives. Many men did not like begging until their need was great, thus it was 31st July before Sergeant Maloney wrote from Minden PoW Camp:

Dear Mr Mayor
I have been a prisoner of war since February 17th and up to date have received one packet of bread, biscuits and two loaves from Copenhagen. I am here with Sgt R.P. Brown, on whom I am absolutely dependent, even for toilet necessaries, consequently his parcels are finished before his next parcel is due, so I would be very grateful if you could arrange the usual regular supply of parcels through the Central [Prisoners of War] *Committee.*[102]

In France the British spring offensive at Arras and Vimy began well on 9th April, with most of Vimy Ridge stormed by the Canadian Corps and some excellent progress made by British Divisions east and south of Arras. Amongst those was the 56th Division, with the 1/13th Kensingtons, back at full strength, taking all objectives and capturing Neuville-Vitasse, plus one hundred prisoners, six machine guns, two heavy mortars and two *grenatenwerfern*. It had cost them five officers and 123 other ranks, but it had been their most successful day's fighting in France.

For the next few days there was an extraordinary optimism in the British camp, that *now we were on our way*. Unfortunately it was a false dawn; the Germans withdrew to prepared positions (the Oppy-Méricourt Line) that they were not going to give up easily. The 22nd Fusiliers were to find this out on 29th April. 2nd Division, still low in numbers after February's battles, found themselves attacking next to the Canadians on 28th April. The latter were strong enough to take Arleux and 5th Brigade, attacking on the left of 2nd Division beside the Canadians, also performed well. 6th Brigade (the 17th Middlesex and the 13th Essex) assaulted Oppy Wood with great gallantry, with some troops getting into the village behind. The battalions were just too weak to hold on to their gains and a skilful enemy routed first one then the other.

99 Brigade were told that they were going to have to go back and attack Oppy Wood early the next morning, with no time for any reconnaissance. On the left the Royal Berks found the wire reasonably cut and made good progress but, like the 17th Middlesex the day before, the further they got, the weaker they became and after resisting six or seven determined attacks by the Germans, were driven back to the British lines. Next to them the 22nd Fusiliers were mostly mown down in front of uncut wire: Second Lieutenant Palmer found a shell hole in the German wire and, staying there until night, was the only survivor of his platoon. On their extreme right, Second Lieutenant Jeffcoat found a gap, got into the German line with a few men, and bombed down it to the right, eventually getting in touch with men from the next division, who enthusiastically joined in the impromptu attack. He got word back to Colonel Barker, who was able to send up to them men of the 23rd Royal Fusiliers, with bombs and ammunition. Eventually the motley crew, comprised of several regiments, bombed back down to the left (where the Germans had retaken some of their

Colonel Barker telling Mayor Davison that his battalion had been decimated, with only 40 men coming out of battle with him. (B)

April 30

My dear Willie

Only a line. I will write when I have time. Got safely out of battle this morning. The Regt does'nt now exist. Only 40 men returned with me, but I hope to find about another 60 or so which got mixed with other units. Palmer V C only officer returned except the quarter. Dear old gregg I am afraid got a mortal one – they fought & died as heroes. The old Regt cant be rebuilt, so if I have time I shall have to make a new one.

The Oppy Cross as it is now, hanging in a dark corner of St Mary Abbots Church on Kensington High Street. (A)

The Oppy Cross to commemorate those who had died at Oppy (the true number of deaths is more than double this, but most of the others were still 'Missing' when the Cross was carved). (Mufti)

line) and were able to hand over 800–1000 yards of German trench, but not before poor Jeffcoat had been mortally wounded.

For the 22nd Royal Fusiliers the whole battle was a disaster: of 240 men that went into the fight, two thirds of them (163, plus nine out of twelve officers) became casualties. All twelve battalions in the Division were now very weak, but the 22nd Fusiliers were weakest of all. A few days later they lost another twenty in an attack on 3rd May. Effectively the Battalion was destroyed. As happened to the 1/13th Kensingtons in 1916, the 22nd Fusiliers (and the rest of the Division) were sent back to a quiet area (the place where they had first gone into the trenches, ie Cambrin), for recuperation and retraining.

Hammersmith resident Fred Palmer was in all the papers in early April when the award of his VC was announced. In civilian life he was business manager of Erskine Macdonald, the publishers of the *Poetry Review*. Around six foot three in height, he had been raised in Shepherds Bush and educated in West Kensington. He was sent home after the Oppy battle to recover from some severe head pains. He recovered well in hospital in Camberwell and this meant that he would be available to receive his medal in person from the king. Fearless in front of the enemy, he was much less comfortable playing the part of hero, as he told the Mayor:

Second Lieutenant Fred Palmer VC, with his officer's uniform and rank badges still new and shiny. (B)

> *I hear rumours of my having to attend the Investiture at Hyde Park on June 2nd. The thought of this ordeal is sufficient to make me tremble.*
> *If it would be convenient to you, I should like to make a visit to you one of my first pleasures on leaving hospital.*
> *Yours respectfully*
> *FW Palmer 2nd Lieutenant*[103]

YMCA Hut Day. (May 23rd, B)

But the ceremony seemed to have passed off satisfactorily. The next we hear of Palmer, he and his wife were having supper with Mayor Davison and he was being asked by the Borough of Hammersmith to sign its Roll of Honour – an honour hitherto reserved for crowned heads, ambassadors and the like.[104]

On 30th May another cycle of events came quietly to an end at Buckingham Palace when Sir Ernest Shackleton, having brought himself and nearly all of his men back safely from the South Polar area via an extraordinary series of adventures, returned to the king the Union

The Foundling Girls were always praised for their marching on Empire Day (May 24th). (B)

Flag that the monarch had loaned him for the expedition. No mention was made about Mrs Popplewell's golliwogs.[105]

Hammersmith was one of the pioneer boroughs in setting up a Municipal Kitchen. Their site at Shepherds Bush had provided almost 8,800 meals at prices between 1d and 3d in the six weeks since 1st May. The next step was to use a larger site, such as the Public Baths at Lime Grove, and distribute the food to six satellite sites around the Borough.[106]

It was the end of July before Kensington War Savings Committee opened 'The Black Cat Kitchen' in Ladbroke Grove. Mayor Davison opened the establishment, sipped the soup (doubtless with a smile), but could not quite rough it enough to taste the meat turnover: which he 'put carefully away for a more convenient time'. Mayoral delicacies aside, the whole of the first day's food was snapped up in no time. There was no doubt that these services were much needed in the present climate of shortages.

In early summer, Kensington Gardens experienced a rise in tourist numbers, put down to doctors and nurses from our new American allies having a day or two to spare before going on to the front. Yet visitors

Hands off the people's food says the sign, at a Food Protest meeting in Hyde Park, aimed at food profiteers and their artificially high prices. (Peel, How)

Substituting meat for bread was something only possible in richer households! (KN)

Kensington Palace: too plain for the American visitors. (p-c, A)

were often disappointed with Kensington Palace – it just was not a grand enough building. The *Kensington News's* Carillon said:

A number of strangers on [Bank Holiday] *Monday asked me to direct them to the Palace when they were in fact looking at and standing within a couple of yards of it.*

On 8th June the large headline said 'Torpedoed!' and went on:

The Premier has stated that the submarine menace is being dealt with but further loss of food ships is inevitable. It is wise, therefore, to choose as much as possible food that is not brought from overseas. And remember that if you are eating less now your health will suffer unless that little is the best.[107]

Short & Sons telling the blunt truth. (KN)

One could learn more about how the U-boat campaign was affecting our food supply and what to do about it, from an advertisement from a well-known Notting Hill butcher and grocer (Short & Sons), than one did from any of the politicians! It is true that numbers of ships lost – very high in February through April – had begun to come down after the adoption of the convoy system. The Government was also urging everyone to cut down the amount of bread eaten by a quarter to minimise wheat imports. In the rarefied circles in which Lord Davenport moved then this might have been sensible advice, but had he but glanced at Mrs Pember Reeves' excellent *Round About a Pound a Week*, he would have realised that in many working class areas, such as North Kensington, bread was the dominant part of their diet: less bread meant less food.

The shortage of men in France meant that the 41–50 age group was now liable for military service. Mr Bushman (supposedly aged '47 and a bit') was of course one of the first to put his name forward, and was seen in the next week's cartoon showing off his new khaki uniform. It stated:

> *Mr Bushman having joined up, it is not in the National Interest that his exploits shall be published further for the present, particularly as he is on most important Army work somewhere in ...*[108]

On Saturday 16th June, between 5 and 7 pm, Kensington experienced an extraordinary rain storm, focused on the north and centre of the Borough (rainfall up to 4.5 inches, compared to just over an inch in the south), which resulted in considerable flooding along Kensington High Street, and streams running down Campden Hill 'like a deluge'. Basements in Notting Hill and North Kensington were flooded out and many poor people lost their beds. In the Poor Law Institution in Marloes Road, sewage-contaminated flood water damaged 1,070 pounds of tea, which had to be destroyed. One dead woman was said to have floated out through a window. Underground stations were closed. Wood Lane (leading north from Shepherds Bush) was impassable for up to a mile. In those areas of Kensington High Street with wood paving on the pavement, the wood had swollen up, raising the level of the pavement in some areas by two or three feet.

Censorship about German air raids was strict – Alan Burgoyne MP (invalided out of his battalion in early 1916, had recovered and was now Hon. Secretary to the Parliamentary Air Committee) had been complaining bitterly about this – thus in the *Kensington News* edition that followed the first German daylight air raid on London on 13th June, there was lots of talk about reprisals against the Germans – but *why* had been censored out. It was something to do with the 'sinister group of giant mosquitoes sweeping in close formation' seen by Vera Brittain at her parents' flat in Oakwood Court, just off Addison Road.

Dorothy Peel had just boarded an omnibus at the Brompton Oratory close to her home on her way to the Ministry of Food building at Grosvenor House (midway up Park Lane):

> *Presently I observed that the conductor was clinging to the staircase and peering up into the sky, and that the people on the*

Conscription is extended to 41–50s, so Mr Bushman joins up. (KN)

pavement were staring too. One man, walking head in air, fell into the gutter. "What is happening?" I asked the conductor.

"Look out there and you'll soon see," he replied, and, looking, I saw a cloud of aeroplanes. Then the guns began. There appeared to be about thirty large black planes travelling slowly and a larger number of smaller planes flying faster. Some of them seemed to drop out of the clouds and began firing at the larger planes, which continued in formation, led by one well ahead of the main body.

She got off the bus and made a bee-line for Hyde Park House, used by the Admiralty, with a shelter in its basement:

I ran into it and made for the steps leading to the basement. By this time the noise was deafening. The basement was packed with women clerks, some of them crying hysterically. One of them seized my arm "Oh, I am going to be killed, I am going to be killed," she moaned, pinching me so violently that, what with pain and excitement, I quite forgot my manners as to reply, "If you pinch me like that I hope you will."...After the guns ceased I nerved myself to go out into the streets again, expecting to see it strewn with dead and dying people, for I imagined that the noise we heard had been caused by bombs. It was completely deserted, except for a butcher's boy on a bicycle and a dreary-looking woman who had been selling flags and began trying to sell them again.

The publishers of this magazine for naval charities were particularly hard-hit, as all 100,000 copies of their first edition were destroyed (but other publishers rallied around).

She had been hearing the anti-aircraft guns in Hyde Park and elsewhere (in addition to the noisy aircraft engines), while many people shared this same sense of the bombers being precisely overhead, as opposed to being half a city away. Mrs Peel's husband Charles, a Special Constable, came across the other problem: on Yeoman's Row, just off the Brompton Road, the residents would not go inside and in fact they brought their children out to see the spectacle:

One woman stood with her baby in her arms, pointing up and saying, "Look at the airyplanes, baby, look at the airyplanes." The airyplanes amused baby very much.[109]

The fourteen huge Gotha bombers had a very successful day: 126 killed and 462 injured, with damage costing approximately £126,000, and most of it confined to a one mile radius around Liverpool Street Station. There was great fury that the raiders had dared to bomb London in daylight and had escaped completely without loss.

As a short-term measure against the Gothas, two RFC squadrons with up to date fighters were loaned from the Western Front. They stayed as promised until 5th July, without any more London raids occurring. As luck would have it, the weather conditions for another raid were next satisfactory on 7th July, and this time twenty-one Gothas dropped eighty-one bombs, mostly in a tight area between Shoreditch and London Bridge, causing £205,000 of damage, killing 54 and injuring 190 – about a quarter of these from people injured by 'friendly fire', such as splinters from anti-aircraft shells raining down on fascinated onlookers. Two other people – one in the Kensington area – were killed from shock at the fearful racket of the 'impending air raid' rockets (three maroons fired at each fire station), and/or the 'all clear' signals. Now it would just be two signal rockets per station while the all clear would be by whistle 'or otherwise'.[110]

BRITISH BOMBS FOR GERMAN TOWNS.

UNANIMOUS VOTE FOR AIR RAID REPRISALS AT THE GREAT "DAILY EXPRESS" MEETING.

IMMEDIATE ACTION DEMANDED.

RESOLUTION SENT TO THE KING AND THE PREMIER.

The Daily Express *meeting and the call for reprisals 18/6/1917.*

Carillon in the *Kensington News* praised the wisdom of the business houses who escorted their staff down into shelters until it was all over. For himself, however:

I was one of those whose anxiety to see the raiders over-ruled any feeling of discretion. I thought at one time the enemy would not be content to leave us here unmolested, but were feeling their way in this direction. Whether through the driving power of our own aeroplanes, or having exhausted their own ammunition, one cannot say, but they appeared suddenly to spread out and make their way eastward, for which, of course, we are very much obliged to them.[111]

Pity any unfortunate with a German-sounding name! A lot of 'reprisal' damage was done to immigrant areas in north London – and it was shortly after this that the Royal family thought it prudent to change its

*Boroughs carried on showing
cooks and providers how to make
use of the ingredients that were
available. (KN)*

German name to Windsor.[112]
General Jan Smuts, a new
member of the Imperial War
Cabinet, was called in and
wrote a cogent report on the
Gotha situation. Slowly

*The sort of 'shelter' that allowed you to see
what was going on, which seemed important,
but offered no protection whatsoever. (The
Sphere, after the first day raid)*

London defences and early warning systems became more professional
and co-ordinated, and, fortunately, it would be another two months
before they would be tested again. It was refreshing amid the universal
nonsense about the frightfulness of the Germans attacking an
undefended city, to hear Lord Montagu speak plainly:

> *The Germans had a perfect right to attack London. London was
> defended by guns and aeroplanes, and it was the chief centre of
> the production of munitions.* He went on: *This is a war of nations
> and not alone of armies, and you must endeavour to bear the
> casualties you suffer in the same way that the French and the
> Belgian civil authorities are bearing the casualties incidental to
> this kind of warfare.*[113]

On 31st July the Third Battle of Ypres began (often known better by
the village captured at such cost in the last stage of the battle,

Passchendaele). The 1/13th Kensingtons would have a short but violent part in this before moving away, while the Kensington Fusiliers, after being 'fattened up for Passchendaele' with lots of reinforcements in October, would mercifully escape being sent to the Ypres Salient.

On the first day of the battle progress was good, then down came the rain. The Guards Division was particularly successful; and one of the reasons for their success was the attack of the 2nd Irish Guards. This success came at a cost; the battalion lost 280 men, its CO, Lieutenant Colonel Eric Greer, and its fearless and much-loved padre, Father Francis Knapp (also known as Reverend Simon Stock [Knapp]). The Chaplain to the 2nd Irish was an extraordinary man, normally resident at the Carmelite Monastery on Kensington Church Street. He was described as tall

Father Knapp, pictured in the Boer War (June 1900) – courtesy Barrie H Bertram.

and gaunt 'with a strikingly pronounced princely bearing'. According to his obituary in the *Kensington News*:

> *Silent and reserved always, he could be alive to his fingertips when he spoke out the truths of Catholicism in the pulpit at Kensington, in a voice so strangely subdued, and with a pathos of infinite tenderness, that while listening to him one forgot this world and its littleness in the presence of that splendid spirit – the soul of whom shone out of the face that made one feel he was wearing himself out for souls.*[114]

He had been a padre in the Boer War, serving with Major (now General) Allenby, spent three years living in a desert in Spain, had various posts up and down the country and in France, but kept returning to Kensington. On the outbreak of war in 1914 he joined up – although 56½ – going to France with the 1st Irish Guards, before transferring over to the 2nd Battalion.

Unlike some wartime chaplains, Father Knapp always wished to share the fate of his men; by the summer of 1917 he had been awarded the DSO and MC – testament of a man of great courage. He had just based himself in the new Battalion Headquarters after the successful

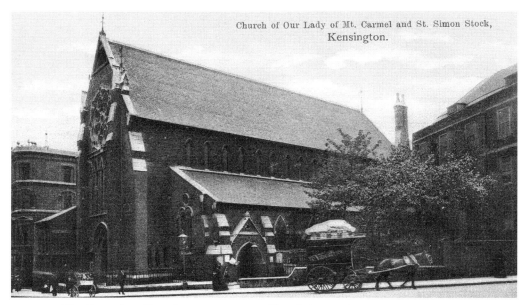

Church of Our Lady of Mt. Carmel and St. Simon Stock, Kensington.

The Carmelite Church on Kensington Church Street. (p-c, A)

advance of 31st July, only to be told that it was too dangerous for him to stay there, and to go back to the Advanced Dressing Station. Unfortunately the latter place was where he was hit by shrapnel while attending casualties. He had been expecting his luck to run out and was heard to say 'It's come at last'. He was taken back to the Casualty Clearing Station and operated on, but he died the next day.[115]

On 9th August a Solemn Requiem was held for him at the Carmelite Church in Church Street, with a Guard of Honour from the Irish Guards, and a large congregation, including Sir Edward Henry, and the senior chaplain to the Forces.

More women were needed for munitions work. The training took six weeks, one got paid 25 shillings a week while training, and a further 25 shillings on completion, which was quite attractive – although the two main training sites in London were in Shoreditch and Brixton and it involved one for eight hours a day, six days a week. Out of 6,000 women satisfactorily trained so far, some 5,750 had found jobs in the industry making munitions or aircraft parts. In the early days it had been more for simple machine operating, but now the demand was for more skilled work like turners, welders, setters-up and assemblers.

Also on 9th August, the foundation stone was laid by Hayes Fisher MP, the President of the Local Government Board, for a new block of flats in Fulham, War Seal Mansions. There were now a large number

LCC training for munitions work. (THW, WI)

of disabled fighting men; yes, they would get pensions, but where were they to live – especially as many would have specific and continuing medical needs? They needed somewhere affordable where their families could join them – hence the flats, which had all sorts of medical baths included. Oswald Stoll, patriot owner of the Coliseum and the Shepherd's Bush Empire, had come up with the original idea, and supplied the land, while £42,000 had been raised by public subscription (often via special concerts) so that the flats could be built.[116]

The National Egg Collection for the Wounded – whose noble objective was to supply every wounded man in the base hospitals with as many fresh eggs as necessary – issued a desperate appeal for more eggs, or the money to buy them. Doubtless this was not unconnected with casualties mounting in the Ypres offensive – not going well in dreadful weather.

The National Egg Collection. (A)

The Reverend Pennefather, when Chaplain to the 1/13th Kensingtons. (TK)

Mr Bushman, as proud as punch with his first stripe. (KN)

In dire times Mr Bushman could be trusted to make one smile (the cartoon only seemed to appear nowadays when it was especially needed). He had been given leave, and was now sporting a new lance-corporal's stripe.[117]

On the 29th August Prebendary Pennefather, Vicar of Kensington and Prebendary of St Paul's, died at the vicarage in his seventieth year after being seriously ill for some months. Not only was he an eminent cleric, but due to his astute judgment in business and educational matters, an Alderman in the Borough Council. He had been chaplain

The Convent of the Assumption (with girls playing cricket in the foreground).
(rbkc)

to the brigade containing the 1/13th Kensingtons in 1914 and had been bitterly disappointed that he could not accompany them abroad.

The Kensington Tribunal continued to sit and hear appeals against conscription. A fascinating case involved one Lawrence, category B2 – useful militarily. He was the Lodge Keeper at the Assumption Convent. His employers wanted him exempted. He was the only man working there and his jobs included looking after the electrical machinery connected with the laundry (there were about eighty people in the convent school), gardening and the lifting of heavy objects, like the luggage of the boarders.

The military representative argued:

'You do nothing that a woman could not do.'
What about heavy lifting? The Mayor interjected: 'I have maid-servants who have to carry luggage.'
And gardening? Mr Stanley Keith asserted: 'A woman could certainly do the gardening.'
The Mayor added: 'We think the work could be done by a woman unless you can show us to the contrary.'
Mr Lawrence responded: 'This is a closed Order, and no man from outside would be allowed in.'
*The Mayor again: 'But **this** man is allowed in.'*

The nuns had been shielded from many of the changes of society; in their eyes a man was needed to do 'heavy' and 'technical' work: how could the Convent ever find anyone like him in the present circumstances? Nevertheless, Lawrence's exemption was refused, with a month given to find someone else.[118]

Lord Rhondda. (Peel, Cup)

The new Food Controller, Lord Rhondda, seemed to have taken an immediate grip on things. One of his earliest decisions was to fix the price of the quartern loaf (around 4 pounds in cooked weight) at 9d (it had been up to 11d in the shop or one shilling if delivered[119]). One food protest meeting in Kensington was ill-attended as, by the time it was held, he had started trying to do almost all of the things they were protesting about. He wished to fix both supply route and prices for the commonest commodities. Sugar and meat were some of the first to be considered; they would now be obtained through registered dealers. First the retailers had to register. Just how many members of the public completely understood the ins and outs was open to debate, but it would become the retailer's job to tell them exactly what to do, hence:

> *Some time after Oct 5th next you will receive a Sugar Card. That card may be taken to the grocer or provision merchant of your own choosing. Who are you going to ask to supply you? Why not make David Greig your Sugar Retailer?*

And it went to tell the customer to register at any of their branches.[120] Short & Sons of Notting Hill were not to be outdone:

> ### Prices Falling!
> *Lord Rhondda hopes shortly to be able to bring about the reduction of the current Meat and Bread Prices. If his efforts are crowned with success the Dealer will be as pleased as the customer. Only the profiteer will suffer. Some say that as prices go down quality will deteriorate, but we know this will not happen in our case. The ideals of the firm – namely, to sell pure food always – and at as low as possible prices – remain unchanged.[121]*

Harrods entered the world of food control with energy and thoroughness, introducing its own Food Bureau on 30th August (soon dispensing advice, issuing recipe cards, making demonstrations and so on). In fact it beat the government to the start of formal rationing by setting its own limits for sugar of twelve ounces per person per week (it would soon have 42,928 registered sugar customers on its book).[122]

Lord Montagu talked to aviation workers in West London to drive home that aeroplane construction was almost as important now as the actual fighting on the ground. He had received intelligence that the Germans were putting an intense effort into night flying. The audience knew the reference – the first night raid over London by Gothas had taken place on 4th September, getting as close as Hyde Park. The solution, he said, was to attack their aerodromes and: 'I know you will agree with me that we are not going to squeal if we have a few bomb raids in London.' Quite how many people agreed with this 'big picture' view is not stated![123]

MAKE YOUR SUGAR RETAILER DAVID GREIG.

Under Lord Rhondda's Scheme the Food Office will issue a sugar card to each householder after 5th October.

The Scheme does not finally come into operation until 30th December.

Householders must register with their Grocer or Provision Merchant, and leave with him a portion of the card issued by the Food Office.

Householders are free to select their own Grocer or Provision Merchant.

I welcome Lord Rhondda's Scheme and will do all in my power to make it a success.

David Greig has now opened at each of his branches a Register for the names and addresses of his customers.

Each householder should now register his name and address at the Branch nearest to him.

Bring your Card to David Greig as soon as you receive it.

The retailers would tell the public exactly what to do. (KN)

Taking the children at a London hospital down to a shelter – sorry 'Smugglers' Cave' - by means of a game. (WI, WP)

Air raid shelters were becoming much more important, as curiosity about the planes changed into realisation about the damage they could cause. One just needs to see the anxiety on these faces. It's Miss Margaret MacMillan and the children in her charge – as in previous picture. (WI, WP)

Mayor Davison was at home in Kensington Park Gardens on the 4th and told Colonel Barker:

> *You will have seen from the papers about the moonlight air raid we had in the West End on Tuesday night, first at 12 and then at 1 am. From the tremendous noise made by the engines they appeared to pass directly over 37 K.P.G., but fortunately did not drop any bombs until they reached the adjoining Borough of Paddington.*[124]

More raids were in store for Londoners very shortly – sometimes called the Harvest Moon Offensive. On the 24th one Gotha flew over Hyde Park and then turned east along the Bayswater Road. The Gothas were back the next night, but only reached the very south-eastern corner of London. On the 28th a large number took off, but bad weather made many give up without seeing London – but there was a panic at Liverpool Street Underground entrance on hearing the 'take cover' warning and eight people were crushed, with at least one dead.

On one of these evenings Dorothy Peel was meeting Sir Edmund Wyldbore-Smith[125] at India House in Kingsway. Her taxi-man refused to take her home as an air raid warning was out. She and her secretary made a dash for Holborn tube station:

I shall never forget the sight at Holborn Station, densely thronged, chiefly with women and children. The girl who was working the lift was quite powerless to control the mob, and Miss Bellis and myself stood by her and helped as much as we were able. One woman was screaming loudly, having already frightened her three children into hysterics. This made me angry and I spoke to her sharply and annoyed her so much that in order to abuse me she stopped screaming, which was something for which to be thankful.

All the platforms, stairs and passages were packed with people, and already family parties with pillows and wraps and food were arranging themselves for a lengthy picnic.[126]

On the 29th they came again; only three planes, but one of them was a new four-engined Giant which sounded like a whole fleet of planes. One of them dropped a bomb on Notting Hill (which must have been very close to the Mayor's house at Kensington Park Gardens), while falling anti-aircraft shells killed people in Shepherds Bush and Chiswick. On the 30th six aircraft reached north and east London but did not do much damage. On 1st October 6 Gothas reached London and one bomb fell into the Serpentine in Hyde Park, with others falling

South Kensington Station before the war. (p-c, A)

South Kensington Station

on Pimlico and Belgravia. These raids, so close together, had a considerable effect on residents' nerves; production at Woolwich Arsenal was down quite a bit, while as many as 300,000 Londoners were now using Underground Stations as shelters.

Many stations were, like Holborn, overcrowded and with occasional panics, while some shelters had introduced interesting ways of keeping people calm. Harrods, for example, used to have concerts in its deep basement. On the other hand, South Kensington had a reputation as one of the best organised stations. It kept two of its burliest members of staff up at the top of the stairs to turn away anyone trying to bring in boxes or chairs. It had its own Nursery platform where the children were laid down in two rows with a space in between as a passageway, and then encouraged to sleep. Heaven help anyone who made too much noise, as they were ejected. Everyone was encouraged to sit or lie down (less likely to panic if there was a sudden noise).[127]

At a special meeting of London Mayors, three resolutions were passed:

1 That the day system of warnings should be extended through the night.
2 That an air offensive on the largest possible scale should be undertaken forthwith against the Germans cities and towns without distinction.
3 That the air services of the country should be unified and placed under one responsible head.

General Smuts announced the government's response to the demands from all sides for reprisals: 'We are reluctantly forced to apply to him the bombing policy which he has applied to us.' Doubtless if this had been a packed public meeting there would have been thunderous and sustained applause. There was the slight problem that we did not have large numbers of long range bombers to pulverise German cities and if we had switched aircraft manufacture over to production of them, it

YOUR OBLIGATIO

YOU have a two-fold duty to perf those whom you have sent to fig Firstly, to help the State to p'ov immediate necessities, and after the to help those dear to you to start in c can meet both these obligations by to your country now. The save grows in value as the time is the National obligation to-day to in

NATIONA WAR BOND.
OR
War Savings Certific
Full particulars from your
Local War Savings Com-
mittee or Association.

Issued by
THE NATIONAL WAR SAVINGS COMMI

One's obligations seemed to increasing in every direction (KN)

Earley's advertisements used to have a friendly slogan. (KN)

But coal needed a form now. (KN)

would have been a backwards step in the prosecution of the war. At present the British had pushed the Germans back at Ypres in three big hammer blows in reasonably dry weather, on 20th and 27th September and 4th October. The enemy was believed to be tottering; unfortunately by the time the next hammer blow happened, on the 9th, General Weather had intervened again and all the Allied impetus was dissipated in the mud.

Philip de Laszlo was an eminent artist, accustomed to painting royalty and the aristocracy, like Pope Leo XIII and several members of the German Royal Family, while one of his most colourful and endearing paintings was a portrait of Viscountess Castlereagh (1913). Hungarian born, he married Lucy Guinness and moved to London in 1907, with a house in Palace Gate and a studio in Campden Hill Road. He received the MVO from King Edward VII; his last two sons were born in London, and he had applied to become a naturalised

Philip de Laszlo. (WC)

British subject before the war began. Yet he was interned as an enemy alien, and his appeal was rejected on October 17th. In fact he did send letters and money through a Dutch intermediary to his mother in Hungary: noble, but illegal. He was remanded in solitary confinement in Brixton Prison until the appeal, then moved to Holloway Internment Camp (Islington Institution).[128]

Carillon, in the local paper, warned on 19th October that the time of the hunter's moon was approaching, perfect for raiders. That very night London was hit by one of the new Height-Climber Zeppelins, L45. Originally having Sheffield as its target, the airship was driven south, until its commander recognised a large concentration of dim

LCC all–women ambulance team – but now with added steel helmets for protection against bombs and splinters. (THW)

lights and realised that it was London. It was so high that no one appears to have heard it. Approaching London from Hendon, he came down south-east approximately along the Edgware Road, dropping small bombs all the way but reserving his biggest bomb (660 pounds) for Piccadilly: that bomb alone, outside Swan & Edgar, caused twenty-five casualties. The airship was damaged and came down in southern France and was destroyed by its crew. It would be the last Zeppelin raid on London.[129]

Unlike daytime raids, where the warning could come through noisy maroons, at night it was more likely to be a policeman bearing a sign. Carillon commented:

> *The "take-cover" indicator as displayed by the policemen who ride swiftly along on bicycles is not seen by many in the main streets, and in the side streets by no one.*

The Cabinet did consider the matter but thought more alarm and panic would arise, with people rushing out

A more inefficient method could scarcely be devised! (Pageant)

into the open instead of staying in their homes, where they were safer. This ignored the plight of those caught outside. In the last raid people had sheltered under the railway arcade in the High Street, right next to some huge windows, which was no shelter at all. Later on, some churches and schools were opened – the latter only if it was a school day and outside school hours.[130]

One could still laugh about it, though. Charles Cooper, a grocer from the Uxbridge Road at Shepherd's Bush, was summoned for showing a light on the evening of 3rd November. He said he did not notice that a light was showing as he was arguing with customers about sugar and tea:

> *Mr de Grey (magistrate): Yes, I expect you have a good many arguments.*
> *Defendant: Certainly, when you have to give them 2 oz of tea instead of 2 lbs, so as to make it go around. As a matter of fact it was only a small light that filtered through.*
> *Mr de Grey: Yes, but a number of small lights make a big blaze, and the man in the sky looks down and says, "Hullo! There's a good light," and then bang! And all your tea and sugar and limbs are scattered all over the place. (Laughter.)*
> *Defendant was fined 20 shillings.*[131]

The 2/13th Kensingtons sailed from Salonika to the Palestine front, where General Allenby was in command, in July, and on 31st October saw their first major action, in a successful attack on the defences of Beersheba in which Lieutenant LC Gates (another son of Alderman Gates) won the MC. In addition, Sergeant WH Godfrey won the MM for an excellent piece of work in which not only were two troublesome Turkish guns silenced, but his platoon managed to capture the guns and kill most of the crews. Beersheba was duly taken. A week later the Kensingtons were involved in a textbook over-the-top attack against Turkish positions at Kauwukah, carrying their objectives after an intense and scary twenty minutes. Colonel Mackenzie was a very proud man:

Lieutenant LC Gates MC. (TK)

General Allenby in Jerusalem. (CHW)

> *My Battalion has made a name for itself, second to none in this Army…The men are splendid and I love them all…Hoping to have a decent wash today; the men have had none since we started.*[132]

The British forces kept pressing forward and the Turkish forces kept resisting briefly, then slipping away at the last minute. Soon the British forces were just a few miles from Jerusalem. On the night of 7th/8th of December they faced their toughest resistance, as they, along with the 2/14th London Scottish, attempted to storm up stubbornly defended hills to the west of Jerusalem on a pitch-black night of incessant rain.

It was touch and go, and many counter-attacks had to be resisted. Next day other units took the last hill and the Turks fled from Jerusalem that night. General Allenby then made his famous entrance on foot to the city on the 11th.[133]

On 18th November, at around six o'clock, there was a huge fire at the coal depot on the railway sidings close to Kensington High Street. Some 400 tons of winter stocks of coal were consumed (total cost of the coal and damage came to £12,000). Of course, members of the public were more concerned about getting a good view of the spectacle; it was best from the station platforms, and the supply of 1d platform tickets nearly sold out. At one stage arches of the roof collapsed and pieces of wood were thrown hundreds of feet into the air – which made them look like rockets: rumour had it that enemy aliens were signalling to the Germans or, worse, that they had caused it as an act of sabotage. The firemen's report simply said it was due to spontaneous combustion.[134]

The new CO of the 22nd Royal Fusiliers, Lieutenant-Colonel Phythian-Adams (pictured in 1915. P-A)

Unlike the 1/13th Kensingtons, which was on its sixth commanding officer since coming to France, some staying just a matter of weeks, the 22nd Fusiliers had had just the one. Mayor Davison reposed the greatest confidence in Colonel Barker, and felt great pride in his achievements with the men – and in his DSO and Bar – but he had at last been given a Brigade of his own. Control of the Battalion now went to Major Phythian-Adams MC, with Captain Christopher Stone MC moving up as second in command. These two were the only officers remaining of those who had come to France in November 1915.

At Ypres, the British (and French) on the one hand, and the Germans on the other, were like two exhausted heavyweight boxers

Major Christopher Stone. (P-A)

after fifteen rounds, who both collapse at the end of the fight. One final thrust by the Canadians secured the higher ground around the village of Passchendaele (now just a stain on the ground) and the battle was closed down on 10th November. Bad news had come from Italy at the Battle of Caporetto, where the Italian Army was driven back in disarray by German and Austro-Hungarian forces some seventy miles, the Italians losing more than a quarter of a million men taken prisoner. French and British forces were rushed over to Italy to stem the tide. The Russians were well and truly out of the war, meaning that large numbers of German troops would soon be free to reinforce the Western Front, while it would be many months before American land forces would be in the battlegrounds in sufficient numbers to make a difference. The U-boat menace seemed to have been largely countered – there would be losses, but we would not starve to death – and, although German air raids were not as frequent as had been feared in September/October, and while we were advancing in Palestine, the actual winning of the war felt less certain than ever. Indeed the publication in the *Daily Telegraph* of 29th November of Lord Lansdowne's letter suggesting a compromise peace seemed to express some part of the national mood of 'can it just be over'. It would need a vigorous speech by Winston Churchill, the Minister of Munitions, to restore national resolve. But we needed some good news.

The GREATEST WAR Correspondent

Philip Gibbs. This advertisement in the Kensington News *is simply to advertise his despatches in the* Daily Chronicle. *A sensitive man, he was deeply affected by Passchendaele calling it 'One long narrative of gallant men flung into the Slough of Despond'. (KN)*

At last the church bells rang out, meaning a great victory. In the dry ground west of Cambrai, an attack with massed tanks broke through the German lines on 20th November. There were a few setbacks, such as at Bourlon Wood, but hopes were high of a real breakthrough, and hence the bells. After a few days, however, the Germans were able to repair the breach, and progress was minimal. 56th Division had been employed on the 20th in making feint attacks with dummy tanks and dummy men, while 2nd Division was brought over on the 26th with the idea of making one last attack on Bourlon Wood, but no more progress was possible. It soon became clear that the Germans were themselves massing to counter-attack. This attack, using new infiltration tactics, broke through on the British right on 30th November winning back as much land as they had lost in the first place, but 56th and 2nd divisions were among those that held firm on the British left against many attacks.

Another raid over London took place in the early hours of 6th December. Incendiaries were dropped in Chelsea, but most of the damage was much further east: Liverpool Street, Gray's Inn Road, and Whitechapel Road. This time the greatly reinforced anti-aircraft barrage deterred some raiders and shot one of them down. On the 18th – a 'dark night' and therefore thought safe – the raiders came back.

Jones & Co, in the north of the Borough, still expected big sales at Christmas, judging from their advertisement. (KN)

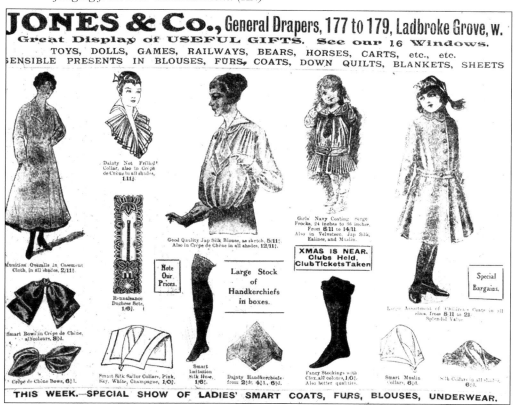

This time a cluster of incendiaries was dropped near Victoria Station with a big 660 pound bomb going off in nearby Belgravia. A lot of damage was done (£225,000), but one raider was shot down by a night fighter and two more crashed on landing. Fortunately there would be no more raids for a month because of bad weather.

The attempts to control both the supply and the prices for many staple foods and requirements created tensions with the retailers and manufacturers. Two examples illustrate the benefits and snags.

Before the war, around half of the matches used in Britain came from abroad. This supply was largely cut off and shortages ensued, much worse in some areas than others. The Tobacco and Matches Control Board decided to pool the output of factories and modify the way matches were distributed. By end November 1917 this had been achieved, and although the supply worked out at two-thirds of a box per person as opposed to the one and one-third boxes available beforehand, distribution was now even across the country.[135]

In contrast, the retailers of meat in the Borough were very unhappy. Supply was becoming very limited (and therefore the wholesale prices were going up) but retail prices had been fixed by the Food Control Committee. Furthermore, carriage costs and the salesman's commission had been omitted from the maximum retail costs. Some eighty retailers of meat held a meeting at the Town Hall, with Mr Thomas Short (presumably a senior man at Short & Sons) in the chair. They argued that because of the changed conditions, 1d per pound should be added to their prices. A deputation, headed by Mr Short, went off to argue their case at the Food Committee, who promised to consider their request and later agreed to it. This was all very civilised this time; it would not be the last time, as animal feed prices were rising and therefore so were the prices for live animals.[136]

As the year ground to a halt, at least there was one piece of good news; Mr Bushman had been promoted to a full corporal.[137]

CHAPTER 5

1918

The great increase in the cost of living press very hardly on the scrubbers employed at the infirmary

Had you opened your *Kensington News* on 4th January a depressing front page Short & Sons advertising headline would have hit you in the eye:

> **Looking Ahead.**
> *We can see nothing but further difficulties with regard to the Meat Problem.*
> *The New Year will probably bring a considerable shortage.*

Meat was indeed in short supply. Across Britain on Saturday 5th January many butchers' shops were not open or open for only an hour or so before selling out; in London the supply of meat for this week was down 38 per cent on the year before.

Over in Clapham, where similar circumstances prevailed, *The Times* correspondent Michael MacDonagh stood his turn in the meat queue only for the butcher to run out well before he reached the front, so he and his wife had to go without their weekend joint for the first time in thirty years of marriage. The next week he went straight to Smithfield Market, but the best he could get was a small piece of neck of mutton.[138]

Now was the time to experiment.

Could rabbits have been the answer? Well, no; this was an own-goal from Lord Rhondda, and it was Mrs Peel and Mrs Pember Reeves who picked up the anger on their travels. There had been so much complaining about rabbits being expensive at 4/9d that he put a maximum retail price of 2/9d on them, with the result that rabbit providers simply opted to eat them rather than sell them.[139]

On the 18th Short & Sons asked their customers to reduce their own consumption to one half of their usual requirements. Formal rationing of butter and margarine was about to begin and that for meat could not be very far off.

One conjuring trick that did not work. (THW, after Punch)

*Short & Sons always
featured a special offer of
the week on p5. This is
what appeared there now.
(KN)*

The caption went: 'Our grocer takes a walk on
Sunday'. (NYTC after London Opinion)

Mayor Davison's war work was recognised. He became Sir William Davison KBE in the New Year Honours list but long before it was official, congratulations came from a PoW camp in Germany, mystifying the Mayor:

> *I notice that both of the above* [post-] *cards are addressed to Sir William H. Davison. Whilst this is now my correct title, I may say I am a little curious to know how you came to so address me in December last, as it was not until the New Year that I was made a Knight Commander of the British Empire by His Majesty the King.*[140]

Corporal Squibb explained:

Last November, we (Sergeants Brown, Maloney and I) had an evening discussing the reputation of the Kensington R.F., naturally Sir you were mentioned and in the course of our discussion the question arose concerning military honours etc, which made us think of the New Year's Honours and who were entitled to receive them. We unanimously declared you to be the most worthy of a Knighthood.

And so Sergeant Maloney had unconsciously added the 'Sir' when he had addressed the postcards.[141]

Hammersmith's excellent Mayor, Henry Foreman, also received an honour, the OBE, while the Honorary Secretary and Director of Kensington's Red Cross Division, Mrs Evelyn Walters, received the CBE.

Such well-deserved recognition probably was of little consequence to you if you were a scrubber at a Kensington Poor Law Institution. It was getting more and more difficult to make ends meet. Twenty-one scrubbers of the infirmary begged that their rate of pay be increased from 4½d to 6½d per hour, while one Agnes Bailey wrote to the institution to ask for some paid holidays for long-serving scrubbers. The sub-committee involved reminded the Guardians that:

The great increase in the cost of living press very hardly on the scrubbers employed at the infirmary.

They suggested they should replace the two shillings war bonus (for war inflation) with a 2½d rise in the hourly rate, meaning that scrubbers' wages would go from 13/3d to 17/3d per thirty hour week. They also recommended a week's paid holiday for those with at least three years' service. Whether it was because the Guardians were basking in the reflected glory of Matron and Acting Master Mrs Bertha Birch's award of the MBE is not known, but the Guardians agreed to all the demands set before them.[142]

Local entertainment venues did their best in these unpleasant times: Marie Lloyd was on at the Bush Empire in mid-January and Harry Tate two weeks later, with *The Whip*, the former Drury Lane drama now

The Imperial Institute in 1897 (The Probert Encyclopaedia. NSDK)

Indexing cards at the Imperial Institute. (THW)

The long view down the Institute, showing just how many women were employed there. (THW)

become the 'world's greatest motion picture', showing at the Notting Hill Coronet.

Over at the Imperial Institute in South Kensington – from which the exhibits of empire had been removed – over 800 girls were busy indexing sugar applications in the Registration Clearing House. Members of the public had been slow on the uptake about registering, with only 600,000 out of the one million anticipated forms received by the due date of 15th December, with the result the date had to be extended until the end of the year. Now it was a question of dealing with all the new births and changes of address and of attempting to create methods to detect fraud.[143]

It was now time to return all the application forms for ration cards that had been rather haphazardly delivered over 7–8 days to homes throughout the Borough (specials doing the job in the south of the Borough, and regular police delivering in the north), with the result that lots of people besieged the Town Hall each day, thinking they had been forgotten. About 12 per cent of forms had been returned because of errors, but the worst sort of error was to forget to put your address down because no one would know to whom to write to get the answer.

The bombers were back again on 28th January. No bomb fell nearer than Kilburn, but one of the bombers had a lucky strike with his biggest (300kg, ie 660lb) bomb. This landed not on top of but just beside the Odhams Printing Press, whose basements were an official shelter. Unfortunately the bomb penetrated through the ground before detonating, actually exploding in one of the basement rooms. Some of the printing presses then came through the floor and fires raged among the stored rolls of newsprint. Some thirty-eight people were killed and eighty-five wounded from just this bomb (about half the night's casualties).

'S.D.C.' from the *Kensington News* went down to the Notting Hill Police Station while the raid was on:

The station yard was full of Special Constables, about seventy in number, under Captain Palmer, ready for the noble work they render without fee. Buglers, in smart uniforms, were there, their bugles grasped by their right hands, ready for action at a moment's notice. The whole station was in the control of Mr Islip, sub-divisional inspector, supported by Inspectors Wilcox and Robinson. Policemen were already equipped with the "all

clear" notices back and front like sandwich men. All seemed to
be animated by expectancy, but there was no excitement. The
conversation was cheerful, but there was no joking.

There were lots of calls. Where was the raid? Had the 'all-clear' been
sounded? Were the people in the next house signalling up to the
Germans? All were answered with civility. The reporter went down to
the basement. It was full of sheltering women and children, being
looked after by a nurse, with a doctor looking in now and again to see
if there was any need for his services. Occasionally a workman would
arrive, seeking to find his family, having gone home and found his
house empty. Much of the time it simply a matter of waiting and
snatching a crafty smoke somewhere if you were that way inclined. It
came to end eventually:

At length, at one o'clock the next morning, after a five hour vigil,
the "All clear" notice came, and the whole scene changed. It
resembled a school breaking up for a holiday.
Solemnity gave place to hilarity and quietness
to clamour. The buglers rode off on their
bicycles, the police ran off with their placards,
and the motors steered away with their
hooters. All seemed delighted that their
neighbours were, for the time being, out of
danger, but it is not improbable that they were
glad to get home for the refreshment and
repose they had so well earned.[144]

Next night the raiders were back. One was driven
to the west of London and dropped bombs in
Brentford, Kew and Chiswick. Not until 16th
February did they return again, and R39 was
carrying the biggest bomb used so far: 1000kg or
2200lb. He thought he was dropping it on the
City; in fact it landed on the north-east wing of
the Chelsea Hospital (home of the Chelsea
Pensioners). Fortunately it just killed five and
injured three.[145]

A diary for each man was the
Mayor's present to his
Battalion for Christmas 1917.
By the time Private Eric
Stevens wrote his personal
details in it, he was now a
member of the 24th Royal
Fusiliers. (A)

Meanwhile the Mayor's Fusilier Battalion was no more. It had been getting more and more difficult to keep battalions up to strength, and Field Marshal Haig took the decision to change from four battalions per brigade to three, with the fourth one being disbanded and its men distributed among other units. In the 2nd Division there were four Royal Fusilier battalions, all very weak in numbers. One of them had to go. Lots were chosen and the 22nd Battalion was the unlucky one, their troops going to the 23rd and 24th Battalions. The Mayor carried on a campaign at the highest level to have this changed but to no avail. In the 56th Division the same thing happened but it was the 1/12th, not the 1/13th Kensingtons, which was disbanded.

Sergeant Bill Fahey had served the 22nd well, winning the MM for some fine work in March 1917, but with the disbandment his luck changed:

Well, Sir, I was with the Battalion when it was formed in 1914 and went through every engagement with it, without a day's illness, and when returning from my second leave I was informed that I had to join the 24th RF, and [in] my first tour in the trenches with them I was captured.[146]

He did record Bill Fahey's bad luck – snatched by the Germans in a bombing raid. (A)

For anyone who could do the sums, the transfer from Russia to the Western Front of a large number of German divisions meant that there was now a surplus of German troops there. To win the war the Germans had to attack in the spring before the Americans had arrived in sufficient numbers to affect matters – even the *Kensington News* talked about 'The Coming Offensive' in mid-February. The British Army, disrupted by its recent reorganisation, was asked to change from a 'they shall not pass' attitude, to one where one kept one's strongest numbers back, with prepared defences in the rear, and being quite prepared to give up ground, ie the same defence in depth technique that the Germans had adopted through bitter experience.

In Palestine, the 2/13th Kensington had their finest hour on Boxing Day when they managed to resist an eighteen hour Turkish attack as the latter sought to recapture Jerusalem. After this, the 60th Division was on the advance again, the next target being Jericho, then across the River Jordan to Es Salt in March. Thoughts turned to capturing Amman next, but events in Europe would intervene.

On Monday 25th February, meat rationing began in London. Carillon, in the *Kensington News*, gave it cautious approval:

> *The absence this week of queues of anxious shoppers outside the premises of the food retailers shows that the rationing scheme is working, at least in this direction, satisfactorily.*[147]

It was a similar story in other boroughs and the Food Ministry told Michael MacDonagh that it was due to better, fairer distribution rather than more stocks.[148]

On Tuesday 26th February – and hence nicely timed with the start of rationing – Kensington's first National Kitchen (organised by the Food Control Committee, as opposed to the earlier 'Black Cat' Municipal Kitchen organised by the War Savings Committee) was opened at King's College for Women in Campden Hill, with depots at Queen Victoria Memorial Hall (Kensington Place) and at Earls Court Road. There was to be no distinction: millionaires and laundresses alike would be

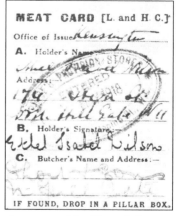

A meat card for Short & Sons. (Pageant)

served the same food at the same prices. It was a meatless day so the lunchtime menu (11-2.30 pm) centred around Boiled Cod and Sauce (at 5½d) and Vegetable Pie at 4d, with Baked Potatoes 1d and a Treacle

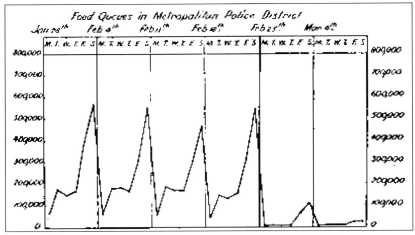

A contemporary chart on the size of food queues shows the effect of rationing: a big drop immediately after the policy began on February 25th. (THW)

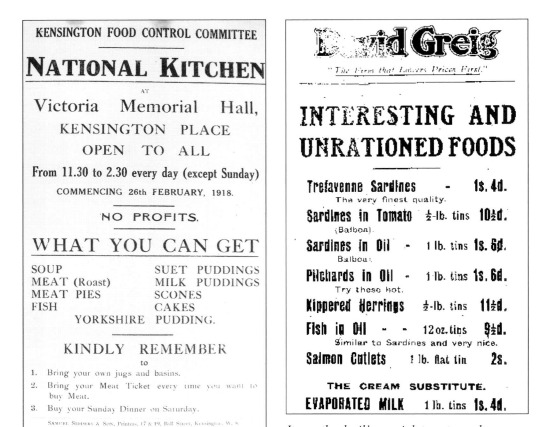

KENSINGTON FOOD CONTROL COMMITTEE

NATIONAL KITCHEN

AT

Victoria Memorial Hall,

KENSINGTON PLACE

OPEN TO ALL

From 11.30 to 2.30 every day (except Sunday)

COMMENCING 26th FEBRUARY, 1918.

NO PROFITS.

WHAT YOU CAN GET

SOUP	SUET PUDDINGS
MEAT (Roast)	MILK PUDDINGS
MEAT PIES	SCONES
FISH	CAKES
YORKSHIRE PUDDING.	

KINDLY REMEMBER

to

1. Bring your own jugs and basins.
2. Bring your Meat Ticket every time you want to buy Meat.
3. Buy your Sunday Dinner on Saturday.

SAMUEL SIDDERS & SON, Printers, 17 & 19, Ball Street, Kensington, W. 8.

One of the National Kitchen sites. (B)

David Greig

"The Firm that Lowers Prices First."

INTERESTING AND UNRATIONED FOODS

Trefavenne Sardines	-	**1s. 4d.**
The very finest quality.		
Sardines in Tomato	½-lb. tins	**10½d.**
(Balboa).		
Sardines in Oil	- 1 lb. tins	**1s. 6d.**
Balboa.		
Pilchards in Oil	- 1 lb. tins	**1s. 6d.**
Try these hot.		
Kippered Herrings	½-lb. tins	**11½d.**
Fish in Oil	- - 12oz. tins	**9½d.**
Similar to Sardines and very nice.		
Salmon Cutlets	1 lb. flat tin	**2s.**

THE CREAM SUBSTITUTE.

EVAPORATED MILK   1 lb. tins **1s. 4d.**

It was the devil's own job to get people away from what they were used to. (KN)

Pudding for 2d. There was to be an evening session as well, between 5.30 and 7.30 pm. The first day's supply sold out at 1 pm, thus demonstrating the demand. Two weeks later the kitchen was serving out 6,000 meals to 2,500 different purchasers and when Carillon paid a visit he was disappointed not to be able to consume the tempting steak and kidney pudding (eating out required meat coupons just as eating in did, unless one was to choose one of the meatless dishes, which became more popular for a while as a result).[149]

'Enemy Guns in the Royal Borough' said the headline, but it was referring to a procession of captured artillery that would take place on the morrow. This was the occasion of Kensington War Savings Week and a great meeting was held at the *Notting Hill Coronet* featuring the Mayor, Sir William Davison, the Right Hon Austen Chamberlain MP, a former and future Chancellor of the Exchequer, and Sir Robert Kindersley, the Chairman of the National Savings Committee. It was graced by Princess Louise, while the Kensington Volunteers provided the guard of honour.

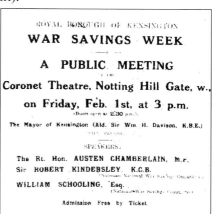

ROYAL BOROUGH OF KENSINGTON

WAR SAVINGS WEEK

A PUBLIC MEETING

Coronet Theatre, Notting Hill Gate, w.,

on Friday, Feb. 1st, at 3 p.m.

(Doors open at 2.30 p.m.).

The Mayor of Kensington (Ald. Sir Wm. H. Davison, K.B.E.)

SPEAKERS.

The Rt. Hon. AUSTEN CHAMBERLAIN, M.P.

Sir ROBERT KINDERSLEY. K.C.B.

WILLIAM SCHOOLING, Esq.

Admission Free by Ticket.

War Savings Week. (B)

Apart from the Mayor, this looks like a waxworks tableau, Mr Chamberlain (second left) particularly so. (B)

The Mayor acted as warm-up man:

Proud at the splendid eagerness of citizens of Kensington... [in responding to appeals] (Applause)...One of the exhibits is a trench mortar captured by the 22nd Fusiliers at Delville Wood (Applause)... As the Prime Minister said...nobody too old or too young or too feeble to play a part (Hear, hear.) Money is essential to victory...[we need to take] personal responsibility for winning the war...Remember, each one of you, to say everyday throughout this week, and until victory has crowned our arms, "I have got to win the war!" (Applause).

The crowd were now primed and ready for Austen Chamberlain to deliver the *coup de grâce*: but he began with a list of things he was *not* going to talk about. He finally killed the audience off with a long rambling discourse about the National Debt being six and a half times as big as it was at the end of the Napoleonic War, only briefly waking up some of the richer members of the audience with the dread phrase 'conscription of wealth' (he was denying that this was Government policy).

Poor Sir Robert Kindersley had a thankless task. But he soon won them over with an anecdote about a working man going into a post office and asking for one of those certificates at 15s 6d that became £5 after a year. No, said the young lady politely, the certificate became £1 in five years. The man, very disappointed, walked away saying, 'I thought there was some catch in it'. Then Kindersley told them that in a nearby borough, savings went up 300 per cent after one of these 'weeks' (Applause), surely Kensington could beat that (Hear, hear). He ended with a quote from Herbert Hoover, the impressive United States Food Controller:

Go back to the simple life: be contented with simple food, simple pleasures, simple clothes, work hard, pray hard, play hard: do it all courageously. (Applause)[150]

Over the week Kensington raised £400,000, no mean sum. News of cannons trundling around the Borough was picked up and adapted by German radio: it became a march through Shepherd's Bush by Scotch

The Tank as War Bonds sales aid. Here it's at Trafalgar Square at the start of the campaign. (THW)

(sic) recruits ending up with pitched battles against the police in Oxford Street and a storming of Bayswater Hall.

A month later there was great excitement when The Kensington Tank appeared:

There was almost continuously throughout the day a seething mass of curious excited people around the tank, which had found a resting place in front of the church, whilst in the Town Hall the real business was taking place. Seated at long tables were many young male and female bank clerks, representing the Bank of England and the Post Office, dealing with all the rapidity possible in Bonds and Certificates. Investors had to line

THE KENSINGTON TANK

WILL SELL

War Bonds & W. S. Certificates

On Thursday, March 7th,

IN KENSINGTON HIGH STREET
(Near the Town Hall)

Investors will buy their Bonds and Certificates at the Town Hall, and then proceed to the Tank to get them stamped.

The Tank: a wonderful money-raising tool. (KN)

up in a queue and take their turn under the direction of the courteous Special Constables, who had quite a field day. Separate tables were provided for the purchase of Bonds over and under £50, and also for certificates, all the clerks being kept as busy as bees. With their investments in their possession the purchasers then passed on in a continuous stream to the tank to get them stamped. The oratory from the top of the tank never seemed to cease…and photographs of the larger visitor found a ready sale.[151]

The total takings for the day were £168,000. Hardly had this finished but that it was Business Men's Week, when another £367,000 was raised in War Bonds, plus £21,000 in Savings Certificates.[152]

On 21st March the great German offensive began, right at a weak spot between two British armies. In the north the stronger British Third Army gave little ground, but the weaker Fifth Army gave up considerable territory and was was driven back in conditions of some confusion for several days. The 2nd Division, and in particular 99 Brigade (in which were the 23rd Royal Fusiliers), was right at the hinge, and lost very heavily trying to keep both armies in touch. At the nick of time the New Zealand Division arrived on 26th March, and the shattered remnants of the 2nd Division were taken out of the line. It had been too late for Brigadier General Barker. He became the commander of 99 Brigade in January, when practically his first job had been to tell his former battalion that they were being disbanded. Now he had been killed in the retreat.

On the 28th the enemy turned his attention to the Arras area, where the 56th Division was located. Some very doughty defence saw the Germans giving up the attack after a day.

Bird's Custard, surely the top brand. (Daily Mail Cookery Book *advertisement)*

But Fulcreem hinted that it was better when one had to mix in one-third water – very important in the summer and autumn of 1918 when milk was scarce. (KN)

The 1/13th Kensingtons were in the fortunate position of supporting others and of not being attacked directly.

Someone had to attempt to change the grim expressions on faces, and Corporal, sorry, *Sergeant* Bushman made a rare appearance, taking his squad of men off to the Bush Empire to cheer them up.[153]

The news got worse in April, as the Germans produced a mighty attack on the British positions in the Ypres area. This was only brought under control by giving up all that hard-won land around Passchendaele. Field Marshal Haig issued his famous 'Backs against the wall' appeal on 11th April:

There is no other course open to us but to fight it out. Every position must be held to the last man: there must be no retirement. With our backs to the wall and believing in the justice of our cause each one of us must fight on to the end. The safety of our homes and the Freedom of mankind alike depend upon the conduct of each one of us at this critical moment.

Just how many soldiers in the Ypres battle actually saw it or were affected by it, is open to question, but its reference to the safety of our homes coming so soon after the Germans had imposed a harsh peace on the Russians at Brest-Litovsk must surely have struck a chord on the home front. Vera Brittain and her nursing colleagues at Étaples, dealing with the wounded consequences of the German attacks, were deeply moved by it.

There was some relief in early April that the peril to the nation had brought to an end the threat of an engineers' strike while, at Winston Churchill's request, munitions workers worked on through Easter and miners agreed to supply men for the Front. The new Military Services Act sought to comb out more people, this time from any industries not defined as essential for Britain's war effort.

On 27th May the Germans began another huge attack, this time on the French front in the Chemin des Dames area. Paris was now not so far away. American divisions fought stoutly at Belleau Wood and Chateau Thierry to help bring the attacks to an end. On the war maps the German gains since March looked considerable, yet instead of Britain and France being driven apart, their armies had united under Marshal Foch. They had yielded territory but not broken.

Appropriately enough, the film version of the Old Bill story, 'The Better 'Ole, was on at the Coronet. (KN)

Even on the far-off Palestine front the implications of the German attacks were felt. At the end of May the 60th Division was 'Indianised', meaning that in each of the brigades three out of the four battalions were sent back to reinforce the Western Front and were replaced by Indian Army units. The 2/13th Kensingtons was one of the three British battalions staying with the Division in Palestine. This campaign here was then effectively put on hold until the cooler weather later in the year.

On 9th June the Germans launched another great blow to exploit the gains of the earlier attacks, but this time the gains were not quite so large and counter-attacks brought it to a halt in three days. Was there just a hint that the initiative was swinging back to the Allies?

Back at home the process of rationing had begun reasonably well in the Borough, but there were more and more forms to be filled in, and the government was not getting any better at designing them:

> *The pink* [Voter] *registration form is creating a great deal of trouble...I understand that in one district six out of eight King's Counsel filled out their forms incorrectly.*[154]

This was preparation for the next election, the first one in which (some) women would be able to vote.

In Hammersmith, however, the Food Control Committee distributed ration books at polling stations, rather than putting them in the post:

> *Therefore, throughout a blazing July Saturday, enormous queues of men, women and children were kept standing in tropic heat at the various schools serving as stations, many of them for hours, while the necessarily slow process of distribution was carried out...And all this transpired in the face of the warning of the medical profession to the public to avoid crowds during this prevailing wave of influenza.*[155]

This one features Butcher, Butter and Sugar suppliers. (B)

There was in fact a moderately serious influenza attack in London with 5, 10, 67 and 218 deaths in the four weeks ending July 6th. In the next two weeks it increased to 287 before coming down to 192.[156] The disease then became dormant for around three months before reappearing in a much more infectious and deadly form.

Vera Brittain had been obliged to return to Kensington to run the family flat because her mother had had some kind of breakdown. She had come fresh from the centre of the war at 24 General Hospital in Étaples where day after day wounded men crowded in desperately needing medical attention; nothing would equal the 'crushing tension' of those days. Now she was back in London, where all the talk was about trivial matters: the price of butter, where to get meat and sugar, and so on. The Kensington Libraries Committee used some novel measurements to show that interest had moved away from war news: comparing the first three months of 1918 versus that of 1917 there were 7,000 more books issued from the Reference and Lending Libraries (not normally related to the current war), whereas the Reading and News Rooms (where people sought the latest war news) saw their attendances decrease by 30,000.[157]

Philip de Laszlo, who had suffered from the reviling of all things alien, was having a hard time at Holloway Internment Camp. It was not just the loss of liberty, but the fact that prospective sitters withdrew, while almost all of his clubs crossed out his name. Eton College not only cancelled his appointment to paint a portrait of Mr Balfour, but told de Laszlo that his two sons' entries had been declined. He had what was believed to be a nervous breakdown and was allowed to go back to Kensington on 14th May to recuperate at a nursing home in Ladbroke Gardens.[158]

Londoners had become accustomed to the lack of enemy raiders, but back they came on Whitsun Bank Holiday weekend, on 19th May. Some twenty-eight Gothas and three Giants reached the British mainland – the largest raid of the war. Bombs dropped all over north, east and south London, but none nearer Kensington than the Edgware Road. This time a number were shot down by night fighters and others were destroyed on the return journey. This would turn out to be the last major raid on London. Reprisal raids over German cities by Independent Force, RAF began in June, as had been promised in the anger of the moment in autumn of 1917, and did in fact drop almost twice the tonnage than the Germans dropped over here.

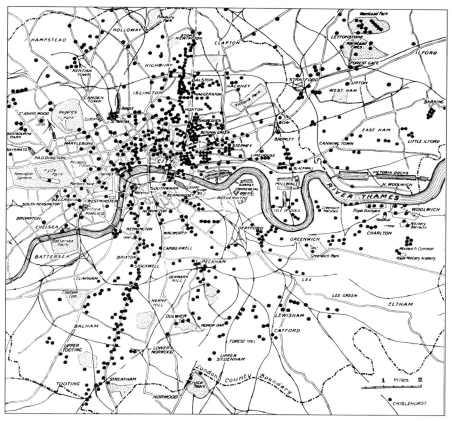

*Bombs dropped on London. It doesn't quite cover all of Kensington, but we can see the main routes in and out of London and the tight concentration in the City area. (*Daily Mail, 1919)

Of all the young men Vera Brittain had been close to, only her dear brother Edward remained. Fortunately he had survived Passchendaele and had been sent to the now relatively dormant front in Italy. On 16th June she read with a sinking feeling that there had been an Austrian attack in Italy the day before, and a few days later she found out that Edward's battalion had been involved. Yet the days went past; and no news was good news. Late on the following Saturday afternoon came the 'sudden loud clattering at the front-door knocker that always meant a telegram'. He had been killed on the 15th, as she had feared.[159]

Lord Rhondda, the Food Controller, died on 3rd July, with overwork a likely contributory factor (he had been one of the survivors from the torpedoed *Lusitania* in 1915). Announcing his death in the House of Lords, Earl Curzon called him 'the only popular Food Controller in

Europe'. The *Kensington News* said he had died in the 'very hour of his triumph'.[160]

July 4th was Independence Day, and the Mayor and Mayoress invited 550 American soldiers and 'a sprinkling of sailors', all conveyed by brakes from the baseball match in Chelsea, to a supper served in a huge marquee in Sir Robert Perks' field. The Mayor reminded them of the calibre of their enemy by citing the *Lusitania* (sunk although it had Americans on board) and the very recent sinking of the *Llandovery Castle*, a hospital ship, whose survivors were killed by orders of the U-boat captain, all barring one full lifeboat which had escaped to tell the tale. He went on:

Lord Rhondda. (TY1918)

> *But this evening, however, I do not wish to spoil your supper or get a bad taste in your mouths by thinking of Germans and their wicked deeds. What I want you to think about is how very pleased we all are over here to have you Americans with us and to know that we want you to feel at home here till you can go back again across the water....So now in celebrating Independence Day the old mother country is proud to welcome her big strong independent American son who has come to stand by her side because he was bred and nurtured on the same ideals of justice, liberty and freedom and will not stand by to see them trampled underfoot.*

DOING YOUR BIT

The Rationing Order has created serious problems for Retailers.

Will you help to meet them by :

1. Depositing CASH and COUPONS with order and save booking.

2. Carrying home small parcels and providing wrapping material where possible.

Short & Sons, Ltd.,
15, 17, 19, High St.,
Notting Hill Gate, W.

Not all parts of rationing worked smoothly; one can imagine considerable confusion with older residents. (KN)

They all marched around to the Town Hall, where they were entertained by a Smoking Concert featuring Miss Carrie Tubb in top form, singing *The Battle Hymn of the Republic* 'the choruses of which were enthusiastically taken up by the men,' with *Annie Laurie* as an encore.[161]

*The king being introduced to the baseball players at Chelsea on
July 4th. (TY1918)*

On 15th July the Germans began their latest attack, east and west
of Rheims. This time the French had good intelligence of the attack.
On the eastern side the attack was stopped virtually in its tracks, while
on the western side General Mangin had a very unpleasant surprise
planned for the Germans. On the 18th he launched a surprise attack
with 330 Renault tanks across the sides of the German gains,
threatening to encircle large numbers of German troops. Said the
Kensington News:

The repulse of the German offensive alone would have sufficed to mark out the week in a campaigning season remarkable for its succession of German victories. Is it too much to hope now that the enemy has missed his chance once and for all?[162]

Despite the news from France building up to a climax, many people's attention was directed inwards. Perhaps the wages of some munitions workers were keeping pace with the price increases, but that was not true for most people. Even in Kensington Council the municipal workmen were dissatisfied with their lot. They were receiving a war bonus of 12/- and were insisting on it being raised to 20/-. The council was willing to put the matter to the new Industrial Council, but the men suspected that this would take many months. Eventually the men settled for 16/-. Shortly afterwards the council felt obliged to put the rates up for the second half of the year, by a large amount: eight pence in the pound (3/10d to 4/6d), but much of this was to cover the large number of empty properties and just a penny of the increase was as a result of the increase to the workmen.

Lord Northcliffe, frenetically energetic to the end. One imagines that Dorothy Peel had gone from frying pan into fire. (At the War)

Dorothy Peel resigned her job at the Ministry of Food, feeling drained and exhausted (she would later find out she had diabetes), but came to the attention of Lord Northcliffe, who insisted she organise the *Daily Mail* Food Bureau:

As that dreary summer of 1918, much of which I spent at Carmelite House [she was using Lord Northcliffe's office there], *drew to a close, one began to feel that the war would go on for ever. The streets were dark, the clothing of the people was dark, for although now few wore mourning for the dead, gay colours were not seen, and the shops stocked little but black and grey material...Inadequate nourishment and lack of warmth were weakening the stamina of the people.*[163]

There was some good news. David Greig announced in a huge advertisement that:

Thanks to the American people, the Navy, and the Mercantile Marine, the British Ministry of Food is in such a good position in regard to bacon and ham that from today you can buy as much bacon or ham as you please without coupons.

Mind you, back bacon was still two shillings a pound – not cheap.[164]

On 8th August, the British Fourth Army, spearheaded by the Canadian and Australian Corps and with French help on the right, launched an attack with massed tanks east of Amiens. The Germans were driven back up to eight miles. The German commander, Ludendorff, called it the 'Black day of the German Army'. Premier Lloyd George stopped off at Cardiff on his way to Neath to announce to a great crowd, 'We are smashing through…We have won a great victory'.

At home, however, there was a problem with 'women in men's jobs'. This obviously did not refer to women park keepers, who were much more helpful to children, who were said to look upon them as friends, while tending to give as wide a berth as possible to the male keepers. On the other hand the unions were very suspicious that cheap labour was the reason why large numbers of women were employed on the tube and in the railways generally at 12s 6d cheaper per week, while discharged soldiers 'could not get jobs there'. Strike action was briefly taken towards the end of August.

More important than these was the strike by the Metropolitan Police. A simmering dispute about

Despite her exhaustion, Dorothy Peel was soon back in the swing of things at the Daily Mail. *(A)*

Something coming off coupons for a change. (KN)

This 'Special', roped in for traffic duty, looks happy enough, but many Specials got rough treatment from the strikers. (THW)

wages not keeping pace with prices came to a head rapidly, with a man being sacked for union activities in Hammersmith (and in Manchester) and on 30th August around 12,000 policemen were 'out'. On the 31st:

> *The policemen in mufti marching in procession whilst on strike along Kensington High Street did not present a very pleasing spectacle on Saturday morning, and I am quite sure they did not feel comfortable.*[165]

Michael MacDonagh got a telling reaction from a striking constable when he asked why he was striking:

[He] *at once gave the answer, "Dilly-dally," and with a comprehensive sweep of his arm to take in the surrounding Government departments, he added "You'll find him in all these buildings."*[166]

The next day Lloyd George negotiated considerable increases in wages and benefits: conceding just about everything except recognition of the union, with the result that the Commissioner, Sir Edward Henry, resigned. He had previously informed the Home Secretary of his concerns about police wages and welfare, the latter had told Lloyd George, and a committee had been formed – but this could have taken forever to report.

Mrs Dacre-Fox looking as if butter wouldn't melt in her mouth, but, espousing the 'clean sweep' position, she stood unsuccessfully as an Independent candidate in the 1918 election. (THW)

Once resistance to the Amiens attack started to harden, the attack was closed down. Instead the British Third Army (including the 56th Division, with the 1/13th Kensingtons well to the fore, although they lost their commanding officer, Colonel RSF Shaw) launched a great blow against the Germans on the 23rd August, followed a few days later by the First Army; attacks followed from the French First and Tenth Armies and the British Fourth Army again; and then the American Army at St Mihiel. These attacks occurred up and down the line and the Germans were driven back to their Hindenburg Line.

Yet just as it seemed the Germans were cracking, at home the threat of the strike weapon was appearing much faster in negotiations. The Works Committee of Kensington Council, which had agreed a rise in the war allowance for workmen from 12/- to 16/- as recently as July, now found (mid-

A CLEAN SWEEP.

Down with German Influence.

A MEETING

WILL BE HELD AT THE

TOWN HALL, KENSINGTON,

TO-NIGHT (FRIDAY), at 7.30.

To demand immediate and drastic action by the authorities, against all persons of enemy blood—naturalized or unnaturalized.

Chair   -   Mrs. DACRE FOX.

Speakers - Dr. ELLIS POWELL *(Editor Financial News)*.
Colonel CASSAL, V.D.
Councillor FORSYTH *(Folkestone)*.
Major MARMADUKE LAWTHER.

ADMISSION FREE.

A limited number of Reserved Seats can be obtained at 2/6, 1/-, and 6d.

CLEAR THEM OUT NOW.

As the Germans were at last being beaten on the western front in September 1918, many were still claiming that our ability to win the war was being thwarted by German influences. (B)

September) a demand for the allowance to go up to 25/-. Since their agreement, other Boroughs had agreed 20/-: the Borough had to offer 20/-.

The German defeats on the Western Front had a noticeable effect on enemy morale on other fronts: the Franco-Serbian Army broke through on the Salonika Front and so, also facing rebellion at home, the Bulgarians were the first to sue for peace (signed on 29th September). In Palestine on the 19th-21st September General Allenby won an outstanding victory over the Turks at the Battle of Megiddo (with the 2/13th Kensingtons playing a part, but the soldiers in front of them had fled). Soon the Turks were in full retreat on all fronts in the Middle East. The end of September brought attacks by all the armies on the Western Front against what at one time might have been thought impregnable – the Hindenburg Line. This was duly breached.

At home the new electors' list was finalised. As a well-known patriot, Sir William Davison was a very good choice as the Coalition candidate for the Kensington South constituency, while Mayors Foreman and Norris were also fighting the election in their respective areas.

Economies continued: jam, marmalade, syrup & honey rationing was to begin on 3rd November, while there was a rumour that Mr Clynes, the new Food Controller, was going to step in to control the distribution of milk, soap and candles.

New ration cards, dated 1/10/1918. (A)

We have spaces for Butcher, Butter & Margarine, Sugar, Bacon, Lard and Tea and two for as yet unknown products. (A)

JAM

RATIONING

of

JAM, MARMALADE
SYRUP & HONEY

*B*EFORE you register, consider carefully the convenience and economy
of Shopping near Home.   Register for
JAM at one of .   .   .   .

CULLEN'S
95 STORES

You will thus ensure *quality*—Cullen's sell the
well-known brands of famous manufacturers

W·H·CULLEN·LONDON'S MERCHANT STOREKEEPER
32·38 EARL STREET · FINSBURY · LONDON E·C·2

*The next products,
jams and spreads.
(KN)*

On 10th October the new War Bonds and War Savings Certificates campaign took place in Kensington, with a six-inch howitzer the central attraction. 'Feed the Gun' was the theme. A Chaplain to HM Forces (the Rev WP Hanks) warned that the fight was not yet over. The Mayor concurred; despite the excellent news of the breaking of the Hindenburg Line:

> *We must lend our money to enable our men to force the Germans to surrender, and then we would have won the glorious victory which would free the world of the brutal militarism which has caused so much misery, and would lead us once more to the paths of peace. (Cheers.)*

The grand total had reached £359,924 (mostly from business houses) by the end of the day.[167]

For those just wanting to hang on until the end there were still perils to face. There was a large fire at Blake's Munitions Factory (making

The Blakes factory disaster. In a quiet corner of the cemetery is the mass grave of the thirteen workers. (A)

incendiary bombs) in Wood Lane on 31st October,. thirteen workers were killed and buried in a mass grave at Hammersmith Cemetery.[168]

The Public Health Department of the LCC announced on the 17th October that another outbreak of influenza appeared to have begun, but as it was not a notifiable disease, the Department did not know how severe, as the only statistics available were numbers of deaths. The advice was to keep warm but not over-warm, take plenty of fresh air and avoid crowded or badly ventilated places. It would not be long before the deaths told their own sad story:

Surgeon-General's Weekly Returns[169]	
Week ending	**Deaths in the County of London**
October 12	80
October 19	371
October 26	1256
November 2	2458
November 9	2433
November 16	1605
November 23	1178
November 30	942
December 7	660
December 14	322
December 21	186
December 28	95

The London (and UK) peaks were in the last few days of October and the first few days of November: altogether around 13,000 people died in London in the last few months of 1918 from influenza and pneumonia. In the Borough of Kensington, according to its Acting Medical Officer of Health, deaths from influenza and pneumonia combined were 132 for the three weeks ending November 2nd (approximately representing October), and 312 for the whole of November.[170]

There were no separate figures for north and south Kensington, but it did seem that the all-causes death rate was, as usual, much higher in the north. Dr Basil Hood, medical superintendent at the St Marylebone Infirmary in North Kensington, described trying to deal with the epidemic with just a skeleton staff (the others were at the Front) as one of the worst experiences of his professional life. Perhaps 900 people were admitted in the three waves (the third one in spring 1919), of

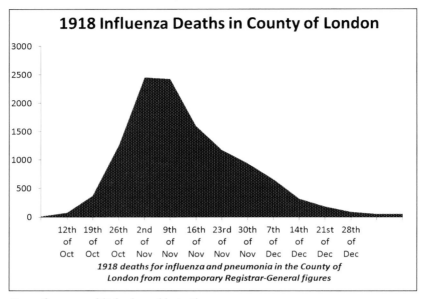

From figures published weekly in the newspapers.

whom around 400 developed pneumonia and around 200 died, including many nurses.[171]

The strange thing in this wave was that although those dying included some of the traditionally vulnerable under-fours and over-sixties, there was a major peak in the 20–40 age group – not only the traditional age group for men bearing arms, but also for women having babies, with pregnant women seemingly having the worst mortality rate of all. Only fairly recently has it been suggested that the virus encouraged over-production of the immune system (the 'cytokine storm'), and the latter is of course strongest in healthy young adults.

The Allies continued to drive the Germans back through October. The long-awaited Italian offensive began on 24th October and within a week the (already demoralised) Austro-Hungarian Army was in full retreat. At length only the Germans remained and they were suffering revolution at home. In the early hours of 11th November the Germans signed an armistice, to begin at 11 am.

At the front there was often a dull sense of disbelief. At home, however, it was a different story, as Carillon noted:

We in Kensington expressed in full measure our joyous feelings on Monday [11th] *and following days. Never has there been such a spontaneous outburst of genuine satisfaction by the outward and visible display of patriotic emblems, as succeeded the discharge of the maroons announcing the signing of the armistice. Almost every building in the borough was decorated to some appropriate form, and workpeople, traders and their assistants, and private residents debouched into the streets and gave vent to their feelings in no unmistakable manner...Those traders who had the wisdom to get in a large stock of flags of all sizes and shapes have been kept very busy this week...* [After the maroons] *it was difficult to serve out flags quick enough. Within a short time every man, woman and child seemed to be wearing our national emblem, or one or other of our allies' flags. The omnibuses going through Kensington High Street, Church Street, and Notting Hill Gate each bore vociferously cheering human freight collected on the top, leaving plenty of room inside for the less demonstrative travellers.*[172]

Harrods' first thought was to thank its employees in uniform for their sacrifice. (The ....
..
..

Dorothy Peel was busy working up in town:

> *I was at the* Daily Mail *when the news came through on the telephone. We opened a window wide and could hear cheering and immediately somewhere near a wheezy old gramophone began to play 'God save the King'. I longed to go into the street but could not, for whatever happens, newspapers must go to press. I was correcting proofs and my eyes kept filling with tears, tears for those to whom peace had come too late to save someone dearly loved. By the time my work was over, it was raining heavily, and there was no way to get back to Alexander Square* [her new home, off the Brompton Road] *than by walking...*
>
> *That night in Trafalgar Square there was dancing and singing, flags were waved, confetti thrown. "Have we won the War?" roared the crowd. "Yes, we've won the War," came in answering roar. A song new to us was heard. "What shall we be when we aren't what we are?" chanted those soldier men. It foretold one of the grimmest tragedies of peace – unemployment.*[173]

Post-War

What shall we be when we aren't what we are?

9th November was the traditional day for electing all the London mayors. Councillors praised the 'courtesy, tact and impartiality' Mayor Davison had consistently shown over the last five years and said they were well aware of the huge debt that Kensington owed to him for his 'onerous and self-sacrificing labours'. Alderman Pope waxed eloquent:

> *That if they had searched London through they could not have found a Mayor and Mayoress who were not only beautiful in their actions, but likewise in their appearance.* (Laughter and applause)[174]

Now one could think of repairing and renewing. (KN)

The Mayor was duly re-elected, as were Messrs Foreman and Norris in Hammersmith and Fulham and, belying his name, Mr Handover, for the seventh time in Paddington.

The Colours for the 1/13th Kensingtons were hurriedly returned to representatives of the soldiers on 3rd December, as it was anticipated that the Battalion would be part of the Army of Occupation in Germany. In the event the London Scottish went instead and the Battalion spent Christmas in the Mons-Mauberge area. Food was in short supply for the soldiers and even more so for the locals; resources were pooled and the combination of expert Army

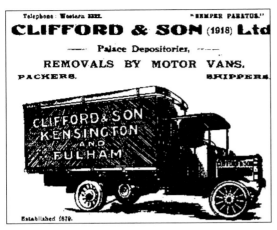

Many would need to move back home. (KN)

You could just about have a proper Christmas, if you could afford it. (KN)

Some normal peacetime behaviours were quickly restored. (KN)

A Victory Christmas, after all—

There is no time to lose if your Gifts are destined for Overseas; even for Gifts for friends and relatives "at home" shopping has *already* commenced earlier than ever this year.

SELFRIDGE'S

"The Store of a million Victory Gifts."

*As the brash new kid on the department store block, Selfridge's went immediately into Christmas sales mode. (*Evening News*, 11/11/1918)*

scroungers in acquiring seasonal food and drink, plus excellent cooking by *Madame*, made this a Christmas to remember. It snowed heavily that night, and proof that it had been a good day was provided when:

> *The footprints of homeward-bound Kensingtons were not found to be in straight lines when viewed in the cold light of Boxing Day.*[175]

Gradually their numbers were whittled away into civilian life until the final cadre of just five officers and thirty-two men (led by Major MA Prismall, who had arrived in 1915, just two days before his father was killed at Neuve Chapelle) sailed for Tilbury on 19th May, and were awarded a civic reception on the 27th, when they were welcomed home by Princess Louise, the Mayor and an enthusiastic crowd of old comrades. The 2/13th, after a slap-up meal in Alexandria's San Stefano Hotel for Christmas Day, likewise returned home in dribs and drabs, so there was no final hurrah of the massed ranks of Kensingtons marching past the Town Hall.

In December there were election meetings all over the Borough, with Colonel Alan Burgoyne showing his usual expertise in dealing with hecklers in the north ('trouncing his raucous-voiced interrupters'), while Mayor Davison got into some trouble in the south when it was rumoured that he was soft on the Germans: it seemed he only wanted

Women voting (and assisting) for the first time. (THW)

some of the cost of the war from the Germans, not the whole amount (as demanded by his opponent, Brigadier General Makins). Polling was on the 14th and the votes cast were to remain in a cell at Kensington High Street Police Station until the counting was done on the 28th December.

On 21st December Viscount French unveiled a stained glass window at the Carmelite Church in honour of the Reverend (Simon Stock) Knapp, who had been such a distinguished and inspirational chaplain to the 2nd Irish Guards, until his death on the first day of the Third Ypres battle in 1917. The design featured the chaplain blessing the Irish Guards on the battlefield.[176]

The election soon followed on. (KN)

Despite all the alarums, the three mayors were indeed elected as MPs on 28th December, as were Sir Alan Burgoyne and Sir William Bull.

Demobilisation was initially conducted via an over-complicated system, meaning that the last in were the first out (those taken from key industries, and those having jobs waiting for them). Riots occurred before Winston Churchill was called in to devise a fairer system relating to length of service.

Unemployment grew rapidly week on week; women employed in Government-controlled factories particularly suffered. By early March 1919 the number drawing the unemployment 'donation' (as it was then called) had reached the one million mark, with nearly half of them women.

The anti-alien prejudice carried on through the election (making a clean sweep of German influence) into the Paris Peace negotiations (seeking to make the Germans pay for the whole cost of the war).

Once the Treaty of Versailles had been signed on 28th June, the war with Germany was officially over and the celebrations could begin.

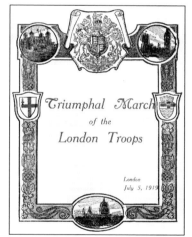

On 5th July there was a **Triumphal March** of all London troops, at which the Mayor's Battalion, despite being disbanded a year earlier, had one of – if not the largest – representation of any Kitchener battalion. Chris Wakelin and Bill White had gone back to their jobs as outdoor workers for Kensington Council, and there is a note giving them the day off to attend (or march in) the Triumphal March.

On 19th July was the **Victory March** through central London for everyone: not just the army but all the armed services, with representations from our Allies, including Marshal Foch and US General Pershing.

The triumphal march of London troops. (B)

But **Kensington** held its own impressive **Peace Celebrations** on 26th July. It featured the 13th Kensingtons, the 22nd Royal Fusiliers, the women of the Kensington Red Cross Division, F Division of the Special Constabulary and the workers of the Kensington War Hospital Supply Depot, marching down Kensington High Street to Holland Park, where

The Victory March. The pennant in the centre of the picture says '1914 Men' – and very popular they were with the vast crowds lining the route. (TY1919)

And here are US troops passing, and paying homage to, the newly created Cenotaph, to represent 'The Glorious Dead'. A permanent stone memorial would replace this temporary wood-and-plaster one. (TY1919)

The Royal Borough of Kensington.
Peace Celebrations, 1919.

The Special Committee appointed to arrange for celebrating the signing of the Peace Treaty have pleasure in inviting

to a Fête which will take place for Members of the 13th Princess Louise's Kensington Battalion, The London Regiment and the 22nd Battalion Royal Fusiliers (Kensington) in Palace Field adjoining Kensington Palace on Saturday, 26th July 1919, at 4.30 p.m., to be followed by a Concert to the Members of the above Battalions at Kensington Town Hall at 8 p.m.

Town Hall, Kensington, W. 8.

W. H. Davison.
Mayor.

The Fête and Entertainment will be preceded by a Thanksgiving Service in the Grounds of Holland House, at 3.30 p.m. Entrances Kensington Road and Melbury Road

Invitation to the Fete for Kensington's soldiers. (ybkc)

there was a moving united thanksgiving service conducted by several clergymen, including the Bishop of Kensington. Everyone, including the Mayor and Aldermen and the clergy, plus less prominent organisations such as the Scouts, Guides and the Salvation Army Band, marched along to a fête in Palace Field, where the Kensingtons and Fusiliers were given tea in a large marquee, with entertainments by the 200-strong League of Arts choir singing patriotic songs in their quaint costumes, and a popular display of dancing by Miss Ephan Maclaren and her pupils. Finally, the soldiers and ex-soldiers (around half were already demobilised) were treated to an Evening Concert in the Town Hall.

What happened to the main characters?
Sir William Davison Mayor of Kensington 1913–19, became MP for Kensington South between 1918 and 1945 and was created the **1st Baron Broughshane** in 1945. In 1919 he threw his weight behind the

Mayor Davison's grave and that of his second wife at Kensington Cemetery, Gunnersbury. (A)

organising of an **Old Comrades Association** for his 22nd Royal Fusiliers Battalion, was believed to have made a number of cash injections to it, and graced many of its dinners and commemorative services until his death in 1953. His nobly named son, **William Kensington Davison** (1914–2006), became a barrister, Mosquito pilot (winning the DSO and DFC) and Secretary of the Friends of Covent Garden for twenty-six years.

Sir Henry Foreman OBE, Mayor of Hammersmith 1913–20, MP for Hammersmith North until 1923, but raised in, and resident in Kensington; apart from the artillery units he raised and the 20th London Cadet Corps, he presented Ravenscourt Park Hospital for Officers to the War Office. He died in 1924.

Colonel Sir Henry George Norris, Mayor of Fulham 1909–19, MP for East Fulham 1918–22, Chairman Fulham FC 1903–08, Chairman Woolwich Arsenal FC 1912–14, of Arsenal FC 1914-27, died 1934.

Mayor Foreman's grave at Hammersmith Cemetery. (A)

Sir William Bull was MP for Hammersmith 1900-18, Hammersmith South 1918–29, and Honorary Colonel 20th (Hammersmith Battalion) County of London Volunteer Regiment (otherwise known as the Bushmen). He was a Privy Councillor, a JP and had an extraordinary long list of honours and responsibilities eg Land Tax Commissioner for Kensington; Principal of the Imperial Society of Knights; and Maltravers Herald Extraordinary. He died in 1931.

Sir William Bull's grave at Hammersmith Cemetery, next but one to Mayor Foreman. (A)

Lieutenant-Colonel Sir Alan Hughes Burgoyne MP had an extraordinary war, dashing here there and everywhere as Personal Assistant to Lord Montagu in 1917, ended up becoming Controller of the Priority Department of the Ministry of Munitions 1918–19. He was re-elected MP for Kensington North between 1918 and 1922. He died in 1929.

Mrs Dorothy Constance Evelyn Peel OBE was diagnosed soon after the war as having diabetes, but the insulin treatment for this was discovered under a year later, and this probably saved her life. She became best known for all her later (social-historical) writings, notably her autobiography *Life's Enchanted Cup: An Autobiography (1872–1933)*. She died of complications from her heart problem and the diabetes in 1934.

Vera Brittain (Mrs GEG Catlin) produced the wonderful *Testament of Youth* in 1933 and several other *Testaments;* was a doughty feminist and pacifist campaigner; and mother of Shirley Williams. She lived until 1970.

Sir Edward Henry was made a Baronet after resigning his post in 1918 and thereafter retired to Ascot. His health had never quite returned to its best after the assassination attempt on his life in 1912. Undoubtedly he cared for the welfare of the men, but he had been unable to persuade government to take decisive and swift action. He died in 1931.

Sergeant Bill Fahey MM, who had left behind a wife and baby in 1915 on the promise that his job at the gasworks would be held for him, never did get his job back ('no vacancies'), although he was released fairly quickly after the Armistice. Mabel bore him a son in August 1919 (the father of the present Bill Fahey, who has been so helpful in collating the family stories of his grandfather). He bought and sold second-hand goods with the aid of a hand barrow (ie totting), eventually acquiring a horse and cart and then a stall on the Portobello Road. He died in 1957, with Mabel following him just over a decade later.

Mr Bushman, cartoon hero, was commissioned in July, transferred to the RAF and then raised to captain. He was last seen in December

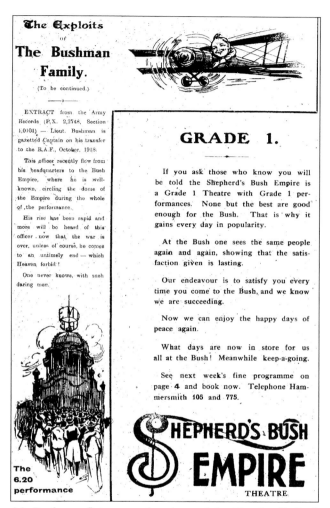

Mr Bushman flying round and round the Shepherd's Bush Empire. (KN)

flying round and round above the Bush Empire, circling the dome:

> *His rise has been rapid and more will be heard of this officer, unless of course he comes to an untimely end – which Heaven forbid!*[177]

Kensington's own war memorial, outside St Mary Abbots Church, and unveiled in 1922, commemorates the memory of all men of Kensington, and those serving in Kensington battalions, who lost their lives in the Great War. (A)

Finally, it is heartening to recount that in 1920-21, the new Mayor, Alfred Rice-Oxley, urged the Borough to pick a devastated area of France to help with reconstruction aid. Souchez was selected (both the 13th Kensingtons and the 22nd Royal Fusiliers had served there). Over £4,000 was subscribed to the Souchez Fund, plus lots of clothes, medical supplies and toys; houses were erected, playing fields created and a clock bought for the Mairie.[178]

Contemporary (1923) picture of the war memorial. (rbkc)

Notes

1 *The Kensington District*, GE Mitton, Adam & Charles Black, 1903; she was one of the first to use the boot analogy; mortality figures from *Kensington News and West London Times*, hereafter *Ken News*, 6/8/1915

2 *Ken News*, 31/7/1914

3 *Ken News*, 24/7/1914; this report was 'Contributed' - doubtless by the WSPU, who were headquartered in Kensington at this time; *The Times* brief report, 17/7/1914, mentions the glass doors of the hall being smashed and 'many of the suffragists injured'.

4 *Ken News*, 31/7/1914

5 *Ken News*, 3/7/1914

6 *Ken News*, 24/7/1914, Carillon (Kensington Chimes) had Sir Ernest ' somewhat embarrassed' with them, but the *Brisbane Courier*, 25/11/1914, loyally supporting Mrs Popplewell, has him delighted with them http://trove.nla.gov.au/ndp/del/article/19998000

7 *Dominion* (NZ), 27/8/1915 has probably the same Philippe R Meny advertising Hean's Essence http://paperspast.natlib.govt.nz/cgi-bin/paperspast?a=d&d=DOM19150827.2.121.2

8 *Ken News*, 24/7/1914

9 *Ken News*, 7/8/1914

10 Very good *Oxford DNB* entry on her, online edition, [http://www.oxforddnb.com/view/article/56783]; 2/9d story from her autobiography, *Life's Enchanted Cup,* 1933, pp 168-69

11 *Ken News*, 31/7, 7/8, 14/8/1914. The middle week had a bank holiday which may have affected advertising, although the figures were between those for the other two weeks, ie ninety-four Wanted, sixty-seven Situations Vacant of which 30 per cent were non domestic service

12 *Ken News*, 14/8/1914

13 *Ken News*, 7/8/1914

14 *Ken News*, 14/8/1914

15 *Ken News,* 14/8/1914

16 *A History of the Kensington Battalion 22nd Royal Fusiliers*, Ed Major Christopher Stone, 1923, Mayor's Foreword (hereafter '*22nd RF History*')

17 *Oxford DNB*, 2004, online edition, [http://www.oxforddnb.com/view/article/36316]

18 *Ken News*, 11/9/1914, The extract is from TB Macaulay's *Horatius*; a longer extract of the speech is in *The Kensington Battalion,* GIS Inglis, Pen & Sword, 2010, pp 13, 16

19 CE Fidler, White City Memories, *Mufti*, Summer 1933, 14, No 2, pp 6-7

20 FJC Pignon, *Mufti*, Xmas 1945, 25, p6

21 *London Evening Standard*, 19/10/1914; *Punch* cartoon 9/9/1914

22 *Ken News*, 18/9/1914

23 *Ken News*, 25/9/1914

24 *Ken News*, 9/10/1914

25 *Mufti*, Xmas 1947 (obituary), 27, No 110, pp 10-11

26 *Ken News, Kensington Chimes* by Carillon, 9/10/1914

27 Kropps was a London company that manufactured in Sheffield and Hamburg (these razors were probably ground there); not to be confused with Krupps, the armaments manufacturer

28 *Broughshane*, 7912, letter from Col Innes to Mayor Davison, 11/11/1914
29 *Ken News*, 16/10/1914; Kensington-born Paul Rubens would shortly become her fiancé, but he withdrew when he found he had consumption, and died in 1917, with a memorial service in Kensington
30 *22nd RF History*, pp 12-13
31 *WO 95/1730*, typed history of early days by an unnamed officer
32 *Ken News*, 4/12/1914
33 *Ken News*, 11/12/1914; later (18/12/1914), perhaps not realising his parents were publishing his letters in the local paper, he let fly at the standard of food in his hospital – much worse than in the trenches
34 *Ken News*, 6/11/1914 and 20/11/1914
35 *Ken News*, 4/12/1914
36 *Ken News*, 18/12/1914
37 *Ken News*, 25/12/1914
38 *WO 95/1730*, *ibid* (typed history of early days by an unnamed officer)
39 *Ken News*, 8/1/1915, also see 1/1, 15/1 and 22/1
40 *Ken News*, 22/1/1915, Corporal RJ Le Ray to his mother
41 *The Kensingtons, 13th London Regiment,* Sergeants OF Bailey & HM Hollier, Regimental OCA, 1935, p214
42 *West Sussex Gazette*, 3/12/1914
43 *Ken News*, 1/1/1915
44 *Ken News*, 15/1/1915; WK Davison would become a war hero in the *next* war
45 *The Spectator*, 28/81915
46 *Ken News*, 26/2/1915 and 15/1/1915
47 *Ken News*, 26/2/1915
48 *Ken News*, 12/2/1915, this was one of the first noticeably censored letters
49 *Ken News*, 26/2/1915, Pte WR Ramsay to his mother, 7/2/1915
50 *Ken News*, 19/3/1915
51 *Ken News*, 9/4, 16/4, 23/4/1915
52 *Ken News*, 30/4/1915
53 *Ken News*, 21/5/1915, Private RE Craig; I omitted the bravado bit about him killing sixteen Germans
54 *Ken News*, 21/5/1915, Carillon (*Kensington Chimes*)
55 *Ken News*, 4/6/1915
56 *Ken News*, 6/8/1915
57 *Ken News*, 28/5/1915, referring to *Daily Mail*, 23/4/1915
58 *The Mansfield and North Notts Advertiser*, 23/7/1915
59 *History*, p14; also *Broughshane*, 4: 6; letter dated 15/7/1915 from BB Cubitt
60 *Ken News*, 30/7/1915
61 *The Times*, 19/7/1915, *How We Lived Then* by MRs CS Peel OBE, 1929, p110-1; *Arms & the Wizard*, RGQ Adams, 1978, pp 118-19; *In London During the Great War*, pp 71-72 (largely his *Times* report)
62 He looks even more 'visibly moved' in the picture for the equivalent march in 1916, where of course the women were able to wave shell casings around. The £3,500 figure comes from RJQ Adams, *Arms and the Wizard*, Chapter 8, note 18, quoting directly from MUN 5/70/324/26
63 *Ken News*, 6/8/1915
64 *First Blitz*, Neil Hanson, Corgi, 2009, p 47; and *London 1914-17 The Zeppelin Menace*, Ian Castle, Osprey, 2008, there were also two smaller raids the night before
65 *Ken News*, 1/10/1915; a volunteer from the Gypsy and Folk Lore Club said that one of his members would want the bear as a pet. The Serb had his sentence reduced on appeal to 40/- (*West London Observer*, 14/4/1916)
66 See clickable map at
https://maps.google.co.uk/maps/ms?ie=UTF8&hl=en&msa=0&msid=10808887788535395376
3.00048bab75d64cc5d0509&ll=51.518037,-

0.093899&spn=0.037387,0.109863&z=13&source=embed
While the *Ken News*, 31/12/1915, in its summary of the year, said 55 dead and 114 wounded
67 *Ken News*, 17/12/1915
68 *Ken News*, 10/12/1915; Burgoyne was next heard of being operated on in hospital, and was invalided out of this battalion in February 1916; his wartime adventures lay in different directions
69 *The Barnett Barker papers*, 3/12/1915, Colonel Barker to his wife, hereafter RBB
70 Paul Destrubé to Marion, 9/1/1916, *The Destrubé Letters*, *Broughshane* 2534
71 *Ken News*, 14/1/1916
72 *Ken News*, 31/3/1916
73 *Ken News*, 28/1/1916; W Chambers Leete, unlike Mayor Davison, is celebrated by a Blue Plaque
74 *Ken News*, 8/2/1916; letter Davison to Colonel Barker, *Broughshane*, 8623 ; there is a version of this in the *Daily Graphic* of 4/3/1916 (also in *Broughshane*) that has been so cunningly censored that all the events happen in random order; you could not make out where he was
75 *Ken News*, 31/3/1916
76 *West London Observer*, 31/3/1916
77 *Mufti*, 2, 8, February 1921, p3, FJCP (Sergeant Freddie Pignon)
78 *Mufti*, Summer 1938, 19, No 89, p9, Sergeant Charles Downs
79 *Ken News*, 1/9/1916 has almost all of the citation, which can be found in *the London Gazette*, 1916
80 *The Kensingtons*, op cit, p222
81 *Ken News*, 30/6/1916
82 Davison to RBB, 15/8/16, *Broughshane*, 8601
83 *Ken News*, 25/8/1916; some of the attack sequences in the film were staged, and the contents were clearly edited to help morale, but it was an extraordinary work
84 *Ken News*, 18/8/1916
85 *Ken News*, 8/9/1916; it was a Schütte-Lanz rather than a Zeppelin
86 *The Times*, 3/10/1916; *In London during the Great War*, Michael MacDonagh, 1935, pp 138-40
87 *Ken News*, 29/9/1916
88 *Ken News*, 20/10/1916
89 *The Kensingtons*, op cit, p240
90 *The Fingerprint Man*, John Rowland, 1959, pp 140-41;Oxford DNB, online edition, Jan 2012 [http://www.oxforddnb.com/view/article/33822]
91 Mayor Davison to RBB, 9/12/1916, *Broughshane*, 8578; there is a slight vagueness about who paid: the cigarettes for the 22nd RF came from 'Mayor, Mayoress and friends' (plus pipes from the Mayor as a personal gift). One assumes the cigarettes for the other battalions were financed by the Council.
92 Paul Destrubé to Marion, 18/12/1916, *The Destrubé Letters*, *Broughshane*
93 *Ken News*, 22/12/1916
94 *Ken News*, 16/2/1917, and introduction of it in the 26/1/1917 edition; *The Times*, 12/2/1917, reported £7,000 raised at the Bush Empire on the 11th, with Oswald Stoll offering another £5,000, so Sir William Bull MP may have visited it more than once
95 *Kens News*, 9/2/1917
96 Paul Destrubé to Marion, 16/2/1917, *The Destrubé Letters*, *Broughshane*
97 Serre Road Cemetery No. 1
98 *Ken News*, 2/3/1917 and 9/3/1917
99 *Life's Enchanted Cup: An Autobiography (1872-1933)*, Dorothy Peel, 1933, p 202, also *A Year in Public Life*, Mrs CS Peel, pp 51-2
100 *Ken News*, 9/3/1917 and 6/4/1917
101 Figure from Sgt J Maloney (at Minden POW Camp) to Mayor, *Broughshane*, 8554, 31/7/1917
102 *Ibid*

103 Fred Palmer to the Mayor, *Broughshane*, VII, 21, 25/5/1917
104 Davison to RBB, 8/6/19197, *Broughshane*, 8360 , *West London Observer*, 13/7/1917
105 *The Times*, 31/5/1917
106 *Ken News*, 14/9/1917
107 *Ken News*, 8/6/1917
108 *Ken News*, 22/6/1917
109 *Life's Enchanted Cup*, p 196
110 *Ken News*, 27/7/1917
111 *Ken News*, 13/7/1917
112 Details from Ian Castle's excellent *London 1917-18: The Bomber Blitz*, Osprey, 2010
113 *Ken News*, 29/6/1917, Lord Montagu in the House of Lords
114 *Ken News*, 10/8/1917, and further appreciations on 24/8/1917; many thanks to Barrie H Bertram, whose excellent piece of detection *A Very Gallant Padre,* is at http://www.greatwarci.net/honour/jersey/database/knapp-ss.pdf
115 *Ken News*, 3/8/1917 for article, ads in weeks following it
116 Ken News, 10/8/1917; the War Seal Foundation exists now, but is known as the Sir Oswald Stoll Foundation
117 *Ken News*, 31/8/1917
118 *Ken News*, 7/9/1917
119 *In London during the Great War*, op cit, p 212
120 *Ken News*, 31/8/1917
121 *Ibid*
122 *Harrods, The Story of Society's Favourite Store*, Ebury Press, 1991, p 145
123 *Ken News*, 28/9/1917
124 Mayor Davison to Colonel Barker, 6/9/1917, *Broughshane*, 8728; the Mayor lived opposite Sir William Crookes, the eminent scientist, now in his eighties
125 '*Director of the British Executive Staff of the Commission Internationale de Ravitaillement, which was the international commission for the purchase of supplies for the Allies,*' *Wikipedia for '*Edmund Charles Wyldbore Smith'
126 *A Year in Public Life*, op cit, pp 242-3
127 *London 1917-18: The Bomber Blitz*, op cit pp 44-55; *How We Lived Then*, op cit, pp 155-56
128 *Ken News*, 28/9/1917 and 19/10/1917, the *Oxford DNB*, [http://www.oxforddnb.com/view/article/34414], also the de Laszlo Archive Trust website: http://www.delaszloarchivetrust.com/index.php?PHPSESSID=7b9585ec909def678741fd348d16b3bb
Also see *Portrait of a Painter*, Owen Rutter, pp 293-324, 2003 (de Laszlo Foundation reprint of 1939 edition)
129 *Ken News*, 19/10/1917 and *London 1914-17* op cit, pp 86-89; Dorothy Peel's eldest daughter Cecilia was trapped inside the tube station but uninjured, *Life's Enchanted Cup*, p 197
130 *Ken News*, 28/9/1917, Carillon in *Kensington Chimes*, and *19/10/1917*
131 *Ken News*, 23/11/1917
132 *The Kensingtons*, op cit, p 297
133 *Ibid*, pp 297-319
134 *Ken News*, 23/11/1917
135 *Ken News*, 7/9/1917 and 7/12/1917; also *In London during the Great War, op cit,* p 247; the local paper reported a cost of 3 for 2d in Sept 1917
136 *Ken News*, 21/12/1917 and 4/1/1918
137 *Ken News*, 14/12/1917
138 *In London during the Great War*, op cit, pp 247-49
139 *A Year in Public Life*, op cit p 61, *In London during the Great War*, op cit p 249
140 *Ibid*, 11/2/1918, to Corporal Squibb, 8653
141 *Ibid*, 30/3/1918, from Corporal Squibb to the Mayor, 8651
142 *Ken News*, 25/1/1918, Mrs Birch had taken over as Master when her husband joined the Mayor's Battalion

143 *Ken News*, 1/2/1918

144 *Ken News*, 1/2/1918, *A London Police Station during an air raid* by C.D.C.

145 *London 1917-18*, op cit, pp 66-80

146 Sergeant Fahey to Mayor Davison, *Broughshane*, 8703, 16/6/1918

147 *Ken News*, 1/3/1918

148 *In London during the Great War*, op cit, pp 268-69, *The Times*, 11/3/1918

149 *Ken News*, 1/3/1918 and 15/3/1918; the National Kitchen was entirely separate from The Black Cat voluntary Municipal Kitchen; *The Times* 26/2/1918 on the smooth introduction of meat rationing

150 *Ken News*, 8/2/1918

151 *Ken News*, 8/3/1918

152 *Ken News*, 15/3/1918

153 *Ken News*, 29/3/1918

154 *Ken News*, 3/5/1918

155 *Ken News*, 12/7/1918

156 *Aberdeen Daily Journal*, 18/7/1918, *The Citizen*, 7/8/1918, and various other regional newspapers

157 *Ken News*, 5/7/1918, and *Testament of Youth*, pp 427-32

158 *Portrait of a Painter*, op cit, 319-41: it would be mid-1919 before he was cleared

159 *Testament of Youth*, p438; there was also a detailed obituary of Edward in the *Kensington News*, 28/6/1918

160 *Ken News*, 19/7/1918; *Hansard,* HL Deb 03 July 1918, vol 30 p 548

161 *Ken News*, 5/7/1918 and 12/7/1918; Carrie Tubb was a well-known mezzo-contralto, who lived long enough to be on *Desert Island Discs* in 1970 and reached her century (1876-1976)

162 *Ken News*, 26/7/1918

163 *Life's Enchanted Cup*, op cit, p 223

164 *Ibid*

165 *Ken News*, 9/9/1918

166 *In London during the Great War*, op cit, pp 313-16; also David Ascoli's *The Queen's Peace*, 1979, pp 198-9

167 *Ken News*, 11/10/1918

168 *London at War*, Alan Brooks, Wharncliffe Books, p 20

169 *The Times* and other regional papers, October 1918-January 1919. The number of deaths stayed around the 30-60 mark in early January 1919 ; there would be a third wave in February-March 1919 of intermediate fatality to the other two

170 *Ken News*, 28/12/1918

171 *Living With Enza*, Mark Honigsbaum, pp 129-31 (the Hood memoir is at the Wellcome Library, GC/21)

172 *Ken News*, 15/11/1918

173 *Life's Enchanted Cup*, p 224

174 *Ken News*, 15/11/1918

175 *The Kensingtons*, p203

176 *Ken News*, 28/12/1918

177 *Ken News*, 6/12/1918

178 *Ken News*, 25/2/1921, *Mufti*, May 1921, 2, No 11, p6; June 1921, 2, No12, pp 2-3, Summer 1927, 8, No 2, p8; in 1927, a grateful French Government awarded Sir Alfred Rice-Oxley the Legion of Honour

Acknowledgements

Most of all I would like to thank the staff at Kensington Local Studies and Archives Unit, who are a joy to work with, as they were back in the 1980s and 2000s when I was writing *The Kensington Battalion*. Many thanks also to Bill Fahey for answering all my questions about his grandfather, Sergeant Bill Fahey MM, with great patience, and for stimulating my interest in Kensal New Town/Golborne and the famous Southam Street (where former Home Secretary Alan Johnson was brought up). Thanks also to Vicky Straker-Cook for her help and inspiration in researching her great-great-grandmother, the legendary Dorothy Peel, and for recreating 'Granny Dot's' recipes in her regular blog http://victoriastrakercook.co.uk/; and thanks also to Barrie Bertram for sharing his detective work in researching Father Francis (Simon Stock) Knapp.

I would also like to thank those editors of the *Kensington News* and *West London Times* for making it an outstanding newspaper and anticipating the demands of a researcher a hundred years on.

And, lastly, Mayor Davison, the inspiration of the story; Kensington's hero in the First World War, and the MP for Kensington South between 1918 and 1945, but no Blue Plaque. Why?

Key to Illustrations

A	Author (and p-c for postcards)
B	*Broughshane Collection*, Kensington Local Studies Unit
CHW	*Children's History of the War*
DG	*Daily Graphic*
IWN	*Illustrated War News*
IWP	*The War Pictorial*
IWR	*Illustrated War Record*
Mufti	*Mufti,* The 22nd Royal Fusiliers OCA magazine
KN	*Kensington News (and West London Times)*
KWHSD	Kensington War Hospital Supplies Depot (magazine/brochure)
NYTC	*New York Times Current History: The European War*
P-A	*Phythian-Adams Papers*
Pageant	*Pageant of the Century*
Peel, *Cup*	*Life's Enchanted Cup*
Peel, *How*	*How We Lived Then*
RBKC	Royal Borough of Kensington & Chelsea
SE	Spartacus Educational
TGWW	*The Great World War*
TK	*The Kensingtons*
THW	*Times History of the War*
TY1918	*The Year 1918 Illustrated*
TY1919	*The Year 1919 Illustrated*
WC	Wikipedia Commons
WI	*(The) War Illustrated*

Sources

Primary/Key Sources

The Broughshane Collection, (Second Series), 7 volumes, Kensington Central Library, Local Studies Section

The Kensington News and West London Times, available on microfilm at Kensington Central Library, Local Studies Section

National Archives online: to purchase extracts from war diaries of the 1/13th Kensingtons (WO 95/1730) and 22nd Royal Fusiliers (WO 95/1372)

Newspaper Library, Colindale, for assorted newspapers used when researching *The Kensington Battalion* in 1980s and 2000s, eg *West Sussex Gazette*, *West Sussex County Times*, *The Mansfield and North Notts Advertiser*, *London Evening Standard*, *The* [London] *Evening News*, *Daily Graphic*

West London Observer, Hammersmith Lilla Huset Archive

The Times Digital Archive, *Oxford Dictionary of National Biography*, *Who's Who/Who Was Who*: available online access through Hammersmith & Fulham online library membership

The Tablet and *The Spectator* have useful online archives

Ancestry.co.uk for tracing connexions for some of the main characters

British Newspaper Archive: http://www.britishnewspaperarchiveco.uk/

Can also access regional newspapers through Find My Past: http:/www.findmypast.co.uk/

To access Charles Booth surveys online: http://booth.lse.ac.uk/static/a/5.html

For Workhouses: http://www.workhouses.org.uk/

Trove Digitised Newspapers (Australian) and *Papers Past* (New Zealand)

Illustrated newspapers/contemporary histories mainly for illustrations: *Times History of the War*, *Illustrated War News*, *Illustrated War Record*, *War Illustrated*, *Children's History of the War, Punch, Pageant of the Century, New York Times Current History: The European War, The Great World War, The War Pictorial, The Year 1918 Illustrated, The Year 1919 Illustrated, Pageant of the Century*

Local Histories

Jerome Borkwood, *From Kensal Village to Golborne Road: Tales of the Inner City*, Kensington & Chelsea Community History Group, 2002

Alan Brooks, *London at War: Relics of the Home Front from the World Wars*, Wharncliffe Books, 2003

Barbara Denny, *Notting Hill and Holland Park Past*, Historical Publications, 1995

Barbara Denny, *Hammersmith and Shepherds Bush Past*, Historical Publications, 1995/2000

Barbara Denny and Carolyn Starren, *Kensington and Chelsea in Old Photographs*, rbkc/Alan Sutton Ltd, 1995

Pamela D Edwards, *West Kensington & Shepherds Bush in Old Picture Postcards*, European Library, 1995

William Gaunt, *Kensington and Chelsea*, BT Batsford Ltd, 1958/1975

Brian Girling, *Kensington (The Archive Photograph Series)*, Chalford, 1996

John Glanfield, *Earls Court and Olympia*, Sutton Publishing, 2003

Harrods Knightsbridge, *Harrods: The Story of Society's Favourite Store*, Ebury Press, 1991

GE Mitton*, The Kensington District*, Adam & Charles Black, 1903; also accessible through: http://www.gutenberg.org/files/21643/21643-h/21643-h.htm

Gavin Weightman & Steve Humphries, *The Making of Modern London, 1815-1914*, Sidgwick & Jackson, 1983

Gavin Weightman & Steve Humphries, *The Making of Modern London, 1914-1939*, Sidgwick & Jackson, 1984

Dave Walker's blog: *The Library Time Machine* at http://rbkclocal studies.wordpress.com/

Military/Social Histories

RJQ Adams, *Arms and the Wizard: Lloyd George and the Ministry of Munitions 1915-1916*, Cassell, 1978

Kate Adie, *Fighting on the Home Front: The Legacy of Women in World War One*, Hodder & Stoughton, 2013

Sgt OF Bailey & Sgt HM Hollier, *The Kensingtons: 13th London Regiment*, Naval & Military Press reprint of 1935 Regimental OCA original

Ian Beckett, *Home Front 1914-1918: How Britain Survived the Great War*, National Archives, 2006

Geoff Bridger, *The Battle of Neuve Chapelle*, Battleground Europe Series, Leo Cooper, 2000/2009

A Cardinal, D Goldman & J Hattaway (Eds), *Women's Writing on the First World War*, Oxford UP, 1999

Ian Castle, *London 1914-17: The Zeppelin Menace*, Osprey Publishing, 2008

Ian Castle, *London 1917-18: The Bomber Blitz*, Osprey Publishing, 2010

Nigel Cave, *Arras: Vimy Ridge*, Battleground Europe Series, Leo Cooper, 1996

Peter Cooksley, *The Home Front: Civilian Life in World War One*, Tempus, 2006

Peter Doyle, *First World War Britain*, Shire Living History, 2012

Major CH Dudley Ward, *The Fifty-Sixth Division*, Naval & Military Press, 2009 reprint of 1920s original

Gerald J deGroot, *Blighty: British Society in the Era of the Great War*, Longmans, 1996

Brig-Gen Sir James E Edmonds, *Military Operations, France and Belgium, 1915 Vol 2*, Naval & Military Ltd/IWM reprint, originally 1928: (Aubers Ridge volume)

Richard van Emden and Steve Humphries, *All Quiet on the Home Front*, Headline, 2003

A Fraser, A Robertshaw & S Roberts, *Ghosts on the Somme (Filming the Battle)*, Pen & Sword Military, 2009

Adrian Gregory, *The Last Great War (British Society in the First World War)*, Cambridge UP, 2008/2012

Edward Hancock, *Aubers Ridge*, Battlefield Europe Series, Pen & Sword Military, 2005

Neil Hanson, *First Blitz*, Corgi, 2008

Mark Honigsbaum, *Living With Enza*, MacMillan, 2012

Geoff Inglis, *The Kensington Battalion*, Pen & Sword Military, 2010

Terence Kearney, *Safeguard Our Flank*, Memoirs Publishing, 2012

Arthur Marwick, *The Deluge: British Society in the First World War*,
   MacMillan, 1965/1979

Arthur Marwick, *Women at War 1914-1918*, Fontana/IWM, 1977

Mixed editors (unnamed), *The Illustrated War Record*, specimen copy,
   MP Hills, ~1918

Alan Morris, *First of the Many: The Story of Independent Force, RAF*,
   Arrow Books, 1968

Captain Joseph Morris, *German Air Raids on Britain 1914-18*, Naval
   & Military Press: 1993 version of 1925 original

H V Morton, *The Pageant of the Century* (1900-33), Odhams Press,
   nd ~ 1934

Frank Mumby, *The Great World War*, part xvii, Gresham, 1917

E Sylvia Pankhurst, *The Home Front*, The Cresset Library, 1932/1987

Squadron-Leader LA Pattinson DSO MC DFC, *History of 99 Squadron
   (Independent Force RAF)*, Naval & Military Press/IWM: modern
   reprint of 1920 original

Maud Pember Reeves, *Round About a Pound a Week*, Virago London,
   1913/1979

Andrew Riddoch & John Kemp, *When the Whistle Blows* [17th
   Middlesex, ie the Footballers Battalion], Haynes Publications, 2011

Jack Sheldon & Nigel Cave, *Battlefield Europe: The Battle for Vimy
   Ridge*, Pen & Sword Military, 2007

Major Christopher Stone (Ed), *A History of the Kensington Battalion
   22nd Royal Fusiliers*, OCA, 1923

NR Storey and M Housego, *Women in the First World War*, Shire
   Library, 2011

JM Winter, *The Great War and the British People*, Pelgrave
   MacMillan, 1985/2003

Special mention for Claudine Cleve's regular '*Women and the War*'
   articles in *Illustrated War News*

For online maps of the Zeppelin attacks on London: http://londonist.com/
   2010/07/wwi_airship_attacks_on_london_mappe.php

Everard Wyrall, *The History of the Second Division 1914-1918* (2
   vols), Naval & Military Press reprint of 1921 original

The Great War Forum is very informative as always: http://1914-1918.invisionzone.com/forums/index.php?act=idx

Memoirs and Biographies
Philip Gibbs, *The Pageant of the Years*, Heinemann, 1946
Alan Johnson, *This Boy: A Memoir of a Childhood*, Bantam Press, 2013 (brought up in Southam Street)
John Major, *My Old Man: A Personal History of Music Hall*, Harpers Row, 2012
Lord Northcliffe, *At The War*, scanned version of 1916 original
Mrs CS Peel, *A Year in Public Life*, 2010 Nabu reprint of Constable 1921 original; also available to read online at openlibrary.org
Mrs CS Peel OBE, *A Hundred Wonderful Years: Social and Domestic Life of a Century 1820-1920*, John Lane The Bodley Head, 1926
Mrs CS Peel OBE, *How We Lived Then 1914-18: A Sketch of Social and Domestic Life in England*, John Lane The Bodley Head, 1929
Mrs CS Peel OBE, *Life's Enchanted Cup, 1872-1933*, John Lane The Bodley Head, 1933 (more commonly available in Wildside reprint referring to her as Dorothy Peel)
Martin Pugh, *The Pankhursts: The History of One Radical Family*, Vintage Books, 2001/2008
John Rowland, *The Finger Print Man: The Story of Sir Edward Henry*, Roy Publishing, 1959
Owen Rutter, *Portrait of a Painter: the Life of Philip de Laszlo*, de Laszlo Foundation 2003 reprint of 1939 Hodder & Stoughton original
GD Sheffield & GIS Inglis (Eds), *From Vimy Ridge to the Rhine: The Great War Letters of Christopher Stone DSO MC*, Crowood, 1989
Linda Stratmann, *Whiteley's Folly: The Life & Death of a Salesman*, Sutton Publishing, 2004
John F Tucker, *Johnny Get Your Gun* [13th Kensingtons memoir], William Kimber, 1978
Lindy Woodhead, *Shopping, Seduction and Mr Selfridge*, Profile Books, 2012

General
David Ascoli, *The Queen's Peace,* Hamish Hamilton, 1979
John R Day, *London Trams & Trolleybuses*, London Transport, 1977

Ken Glazier, *The Battles of the General (London Buses 1918-29)*, Capital Transport, 2003

Claire Masset, *Department Stores*, Shire Library, 2010

Mrs CS Peel, *Meatless Cookery Made Easy*, George Newnes, nd prewar probably ~1910

Mrs CS Peel, *Daily Mail Cookery Book*, Associated Newspapers, 4th edition 1920

Guy R Williams, *The Hidden World of Scotland Yard*, Hutchinson, 1972

Index